Guided Math Made Easy

Grade 2

by Krista Fanning

Carson-Dellosa Publishing LLC
Greensboro, North Carolina

Credits

Content Editor: Amy R. Gamble

Copy Editor: Rebecca Benning

Layout Design: Van Harris

Cover Design: Lori Jackson

 This book has been correlated to state, common core state, national, and Canadian provincial standards. Visit *www.carsondellosa.com* to search for and view its correlations to your standards.

Carson-Dellosa Publishing LLC
PO Box 35665
Greensboro, NC 27425 USA
www.carsondellosa.com

ISBN 978-1-609964-69-6
02-021131151

Table of Contents

Skills Matrix

Page Number	Place Value	Operations	Patterns	Problem Solving	Measurement	Time	Geometry	Graphing
6–9	○	○						
10–13	○	○						
14–17	○	○						
18–21	○	○						
22–25		○		○				
26–29		○	○					
30–33		○	○					
34–37		○		○				
38–41							○	
42–45		○						
46–49		○						
50–53		○		○				
54–57		○		○				
58–61					○			
62–65					○			
66–69						○		
70–73							○	
74–77							○	
78–81				○			○	
82–85				○				○
86–89				○				○
90–93				○				○

Introduction

Guided Math Made Easy addresses the range of students' skills by providing differentiated math instruction. Guided Math is similar to Guided Reading in that students are sorted into groups by ability, and lessons are tailored to the needs of each group. This way, the teacher can work on basic concepts with struggling learners and on higher-order thinking skills with students who need extension. Groups may be reorganized often as objectives and topics change.

Lessons in this professional resource maximize the impact of instruction through the use of whole-class direction, guided small-group work, and math journals. *Guided Math Made Easy* incorporates ideas for using ongoing assessment to guide instruction and increase student learning, and for using hands-on, problem-solving experiences with small groups to encourage mathematical communication and discussion.

Guided lessons are hands-on and not worksheet-driven. The teacher asks guiding questions that elicit different levels of responses from students. Students are encouraged to "show how they know" through words, pictures, or concrete manipulatives. Student activity sheets can be used for review, sent home for homework, placed at a center, or used for informal assessment.

Activities follow a natural skill progression and align with state and national standards. By building on already learned material, each lesson reinforces the concepts needed for academic success. Students will develop a deep, conceptual understanding of computational fluency and proficiency with problem solving, among other skills.

This workbook contains 22 mini-lessons and more than 60 activity sheets grouped by the five NCTM (National Council of Teachers of Mathematics) content strands: Number and Operations, Algebra, Measurement, Geometry, and Data Analysis & Probability. The mini-lessons are designed to be supplemental and easy to integrate into an existing math curriculum. Following each whole-group mini-lesson are three small-group, guided lessons: one below level, one on level, and one above level. Three differentiated activity sheets will reinforce the skill(s) presented in each small-group lesson. Discrete symbols identify each activity sheet's skill level to make distribution quick and easy.

Great for use at school and at home, *Guided Math Made Easy* supports students in becoming analytical thinkers.

Key

Below Level: ◯

On Level: ▢

Above Level △

Number and Operations

Materials:
- Base ten blocks
- Counters
- Chart paper
- Paper
- Pencils
- Activity sheets (pages 7–9)
- Math journals

Objective

Use place value to represent numbers using numerals, words, models, and expanded form.

Mini-Lesson

1. Use base ten blocks to review place value. Show how 10 units make 1 rod and 10 rods make 1 flat. Discuss the term *digit* and give examples of one-, two-, and three-digit numbers.
2. Write a three-digit number on the board. Model how to use base ten blocks to show the number. Explain that the order is always ones, tens, and hundreds moving from right to left.
3. Ask, "What is the value of each digit in this number?" Show how to use those values to write the number in expanded form. (For example, 100 + 60 + 4.)
4. Model how to show and write a three-digit number with a zero in the ones or tens place. Point out how the expanded form does not include the zero.
5. Say a three-digit number aloud. Ask volunteers to build the base ten model, write the number in expanded form, and write the number in standard form.

Group 1 ◯

Reinforce Terminology

1. Review the term *digit*. Ask, "How many different one-digit numbers can you write?" Have students use cubes to model different one-digit numbers. Emphasize that the digit represents the ones place.
2. Draw two short, horizontal lines. Identify them as *ones* and *tens* places. Discuss the options for numbers you can make with two place value spaces. Have students model two-digit numbers with rods and units. Demonstrate how to write the numbers in expanded form and standard form. Follow the same process for three-digit numbers, identifying the *hundreds* place.
3. Have students use base ten blocks to build two- and three-digit numbers. Have them record the numbers in their math journals in standard and expanded form and identify the place value for each digit.

Group 2 ▢

Represent Numbers

1. Say a three-digit number. Ask, "What are some different ways to show this number?" Give students counters, base ten blocks, and paper and pencils to model the number in different ways.
2. Show a three-digit number using base ten blocks. Direct students to write this number in expanded form using the model as their guide. Ask, "How is writing numbers in expanded form like showing numbers with base ten blocks? How do you show place value for each digit with each method?"
3. Show a three-digit number with a zero in one place using base ten blocks. (For example, 205.) Have students write the standard and expanded forms of the model. Ask, "Are 2 + 5 or 20 + 5 correct ways to show this number? Is it needed in the expanded form?" Have students use base ten blocks to support their answers.
4. In their math journals, have students write a number in standard form, draw a picture of it in base ten blocks, and write it in expanded form.

Group 3 △

Exploring Place Values

1. Model the number 2,050. Ask, "What do you do when there is a zero in a place value? Does it matter whether you write a zero in the standard form? Does it matter whether you write a zero in the expanded form? Can you write an additional zero in either form and not change the value of the number? How can you check if you have the correct expanded form?"
2. Write several three- and four-digit numbers on chart paper. Build an incorrect model for one of the numbers and write an incorrect expanded form for one of the numbers. (For example, 4 + 500 + 2,000 + 70.) Ask, "What errors, if any, did I make? What should I change so that the models or expanded forms match the numbers? Does the order of numbers matter in expanded form? Does the order of numbers matter in standard form?"
3. Have students write in their math journals to explain the difference between the numbers 1,509 and 1,590.

Name_____

Write each number in expanded form. The first one has been done for you.

1.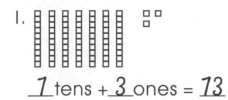

   _1_ tens + _3_ ones = _13_

2.

   ___ tens + ___ ones = 18

3.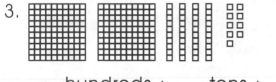

   ___ hundreds + ___ tens + ___ ones = 249

4.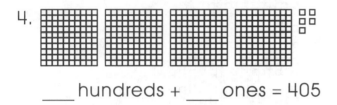

   ___ hundreds + ___ ones = 405

5.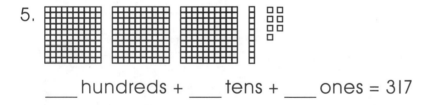

   ___ hundreds + ___ tens + ___ ones = 317

Write the value of the underlined digit. The first one has been done for you.

6. <u>3</u>8

   _3 tens_____ = _30_

7. 5<u>2</u>

   _____ = _____

8. 2<u>7</u>4

   _____ = _____

9. <u>6</u>19

   _____ = _____

10. <u>8</u>01

   _____ = _____

Name_____

Write each number in expanded form and in standard form.

1.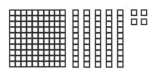

= _____ + _____ = _____

2.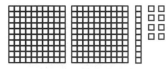

= _____ + _____ = _____

3.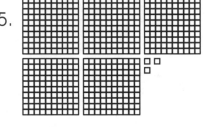

= _____ + _____ + _____ = _____

4.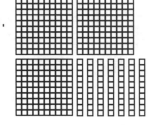

= _____ + _____ + _____ = _____

5.

= _____ + _____ = _____

6.

= _____ + _____ = _____

Write each number in expanded form.

7. 419

_____

8. 280

_____

9. 735

_____

10. 607

_____

Write each number in standard form.

11. 900 + 30 + 5 _____

12. 400 + 8 _____

13. 300 + 10 + 2 _____

14. 800 + 60 _____

Name_____

Circle the matching number for each model. Then, write the number in expanded form.

1. 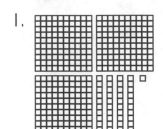   131   314   341   _____

2. 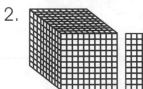 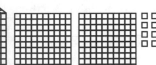   128   1,028   1,208   _____

3. 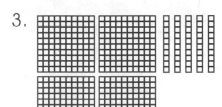   45   405   450   _____

4. 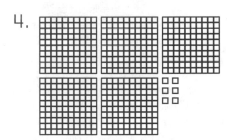   56   506   560   _____

Write each number in standard form.

5. seven hundred sixty

_____

6. three thousand sixteen

_____

7. two thousand eighty

_____

8. nine hundred one

_____

9. one thousand three hundred twelve

_____

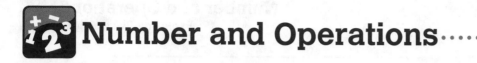

Number and Operations

Materials:
- Base ten blocks
- Index cards
- Activity sheets (pages 11–13)
- Math journals

Objective
Compare and order whole numbers.

Mini-Lesson

1. Use base ten blocks to compare two numbers. Model 3 rods and 5 rods. Remind students that each rod is made of 10 units. Write the standard form of each number under the models.
2. Ask, "What digit is in the tens place in the first number? What digit is in the tens place in the second number? Which model has more rods? Which number is larger?"
3. Have students build models for the numbers 42 and 46. Start with the largest place value of the two numbers. The two numbers have an equal amount in the tens place. Compare the ones place. Ask, "Which number has more units in the ones place?" Say, "46 is greater than 42, and 42 is less than 46" to reinforce the relationship. Introduce the symbols for less than (<) and greater than (>).
4. Follow the same process for three-digit numbers. Include pairs with equal hundreds and tens places. Ask students to identify the larger number in each pair.

Group 1 ○

Reinforce Place Value
1. Write the numbers *45* and *36* on the board. Ask, "What does each digit stand for in these numbers?" Have students build each number using base ten blocks.
2. Looking at the models, ask, "Which number has more tens rods? Which has more ones units? Which place value tells which number is greater? Which number is greater?" Reinforce the relationship with comparative sentences. (For example, 36 is less than 45, or 45 is greater than 36.)
3. Use the same process to compare additional pairs of two-digit numbers. Remind students to always start with the largest place value. Identify the digit in each place and use math vocabulary to compare the numbers. Let students who are ready move on to three-digit numbers.
4. Have students describe the process in their math journals.

Group 2 ☐

Compare Numbers
1. Review place value and reinforce that place value increases from right to left. Write the numbers *28* and *37* on the board. Ask, "What digits are in the ones and tens places of each number? Which place value do we compare first? Which number is greater?" Build each model with base ten blocks to confirm. Compare the numbers using the appropriate greater than and less than symbols.
2. Follow the same process with *156* and *162*. Ask, "What is the largest place value in these numbers? Can you use this place value to tell which number is greater? What should you do to compare these numbers?" Show students how to move to the next largest place value in each number and compare.
3. Explain how to compare two numbers with different place values, such as *19* and *134*. Ask, "How can you quickly tell which number is greater?"
4. Have students write pairs of numbers in their math journals and switch with partners to compare using the symbols >, <, and =.

Group 3 △

Order Numbers
1. Write *270*, *217*, and *372* on the board. Ask, "What is the name of the largest place value in each of these three numbers? Can you compare these numbers using only the hundreds place?"
2. Compare the third number to the first two. Ask, "Which is the greatest number in this set? How can you tell?"
3. Next, look at 270 and 217. Ask, "Can you tell which number is greater from the hundreds place only? What do you need to do to compare them?" Model how to move to the tens place and compare the digits in the first two numbers.
4. Order the numbers using symbols (217 < 270 < 372 or 372 > 270 > 217). Ask students to read the comparison aloud.
5. Have students write in their math journals to explain how to compare 846, 748, and 864.

Name_____

Write the number shown by each model. Then, circle the greater number in each pair. The first one has been done for you.

1.

___29___   ⟨31⟩

2.

_____   _____

3.

_____   _____

4.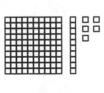

_____   _____

5.

_____   _____

Write the numbers on the correct lines to make each statement true.

6. 50 68   _____ is greater than _____

7. 27 21   _____ is less than _____

8. 43 34   _____ is less than _____

Name_____

Write the number shown by each model. Then, circle the number greater than that number.

1.

_____   62   63   65

2.

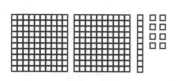

_____   29   210   223

3.

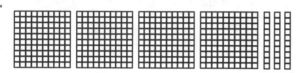

_____   45   403   435

Write > or < in each box to make the sentence true.

4. 39 ☐ 24

5. 167 ☐ 169

6. 280 ☐ 208

7. 917 ☐ 97

8. 426 ☐ 430

9. 753 ☐ 751

Write each set of numbers in order from least to greatest.

10. 615, 65, 561 _____

11. 380, 308, 38 _____

12. 472, 274, 427 _____

Name_____

Write each set of numbers in order from least to greatest.

1. 85, 58, 95 _____

2. 32, 25, 53 _____

3. 174, 157, 147 _____

4. 304, 430, 340 _____

5. 591, 590, 509 _____

6. 76, 761, 716 _____

7. 483, 487, 49 _____

Write > or < in each box to make the sentence true.

8. 342 ☐ 391

9. 217 ☐ 207

10. 1,060 ☐ 106

11. 4,538 ☐ 4,835

12. 2,900 ☐ 2,897 ☐ 2,987

13. 568 ☐ 658 ☐ 685

14. 1,247 ☐ 1,242 ☐ 1,238

Number and Operations

Objective
Add multi-digit numbers with and without regrouping.

Materials:
- Base ten blocks
- Chart paper
- Activity sheets (pages 15–17)
- Math journals

Mini-Lesson

1. Write *35 + 24* on the board. Show each number using base ten blocks. Stack the models like an addition problem, aligning each place value.
2. Tell students to always begin with the ones place. Find the total number of units and write 9 under the ones column on the board. Then, find the total number of rods and write 5 under the tens column. Read the entire problem aloud and confirm that the model shows the sum.
3. Follow the same process with an addition problem demonstrating regrouping. Write *68 + 57*. Remind students to begin with the ones place.
4. Count the total units (15). Demonstrate how to regroup 10 units into 1 rod and move the rod to the tens place. The remaining number of units is the number of ones in the sum. Count the total rods, including the regrouped rod. Write the sum.

Group 1 ○

Reinforce the Process

1. Write *43 + 15* on chart paper. Have students build each number using base ten blocks, stacking the two models and aligning place values.
2. Ask, "Where do we begin adding? Where do we write the sum?" Count the ones units together and write *8* in the ones column. Then, count the total number of rods and write it in the tens column. Read the sum and confirm that the base ten blocks show 58.
3. Write *64 + 29* on chart paper. Ask, "What is the sum of the ones? How many digits can you write in a place value space? What do you do when the sum of a column is greater than 9?" Model how to exchange 10 units for 1 rod. This is called *regrouping*. Let students practice regrouping ones into tens with random handfuls of ones units.
4. Write addition problems with and without regrouping on chart paper. Have students find the sums using base ten models to support their solutions.
5. Have students write in their math journals to explain how to add two-digit numbers.

Group 2 □

Practical Addition

1. Brainstorm everyday examples of people using addition. (For example, purchasing items, making deposits at a bank, calculating the time spent doing tasks.)
2. Write *$48* and *$87* on chart paper. Ask, "How should I align these amounts to add them on my deposit slip? In which column do I begin adding? Why can't I start in the tens place?"
3. Have students write and solve the addition problem. Ask, "Why can't we leave a two-digit number in the ones place?" Explain that each digit in a number can only be 0–9. Ask, "Did we leave a two-digit number in the tens place?" Have students explain regrouping tens into hundreds.
4. Challenge students to write and solve real-world addition problems as a small group.
5. Have students explain regrouping in their math journals.

Group 3 △

Advanced Addition

1. Introduce addition of three multi-digit numbers. Write *87*, *45*, and *62* on chart paper. Ask, "How can I add all three of these numbers at the same time?"
2. Have students align the problem to add the numbers vertically. Review the process of regrouping. Remind students to include any regrouped number in the next column so that the value is not lost.
3. Write *1,329*; *84*; and *567* on chart paper. Ask, "How can I add three numbers with different numbers of digits? Can I align the numbers by the first digit in each number? Why must I always align numbers by the ones place?" Have students align the problem correctly and solve.
4. Write examples on the board, making a different mistake (improper alignment, not regrouping, etc.) in each addition problem. Challenge students to find and correct the errors.
5. Have students write in their math journals to explain how to add three numbers together.

Name_____

Find each sum. Cross off the answer in the bank below.

Answer Bank				
55	95	88	83	90
121	58	165	79	52

1. 28 + 51 =

2. 64 + 24 =

3. 37 + 18 =

4. 17 + 35 =

5. 43 + 52 =

6. 42 + 48 =

7. 37 + 21 =

8. 28 + 55 =

9. 95 + 26 =

10. 89 + 76 =

Name_____

Look at the prices of the items below. Find the total price for each purchase.

Prices				
$19	$34	$12	$48	$69

1. $ ____
   + ____
   $ ____

2. $ ____
   + ____
   $ ____
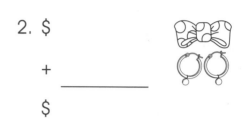

3. $ ____
   + ____
   $ ____
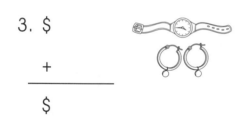

4. $ ____
   + ____
   $ ____

5. $ ____
   + ____
   $ ____

6. $ ____
   + ____
   $ ____
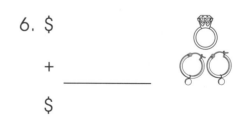

7. $ ____
   + ____
   $ ____

8. $ ____
   + ____
   $ ____
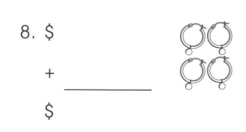

16

Name_____

Rewrite the addends vertically and find each sum.

1. 37 + 99 + 42

+ _____

2. 58 + 67 + 9

+ _____

3. 21 + 32 + 47

+ _____

4. 754 + 86 + 28

+ _____

5. 28 + 7 + 363

+ _____

6. 250 + 94 + 8

+ _____

7. 703 + 318 + 87

+ _____

8. 1,491 + 96 + 540

+ _____

Write the missing digit in each number.

9. ☐8 + 4☐ + 29 = 112

10. 21☐ + 1☐2 + ☐81 = 769

11. 347 + 1☐2 + ☐2☐ = 958

12. ☐00 + 7☐ + ☐3 + 14 = 226

Number and Operations

Materials:
- Base ten blocks
- Chart paper
- Activity sheets (pages 19–21)
- Math journals

Objective
Subtract multi-digit numbers with and without regrouping.

Mini-Lesson

1. Write *96 – 18* on the board. Build each number using base ten blocks.
2. Stack the two models and align place values to form a subtraction problem. Remind students to always begin with the ones place and, in subtraction, always subtract from top to bottom in a column.
3. Use ones units to show that you cannot subtract 8 from 6. Use a tens rod from the tens column to model how to exchange it for 10 ones units. Explain that the value of the number has not changed, and it is now possible to subtract in the ones column.
4. Subtract each column. Explain that addition and subtraction are inverse operations—they undo each other. Model how to check your answer by using addition (78 + 18 = 96).
5. Practice building and subtracting numbers using base ten blocks.

Group 1 ○

Reinforce the Process
1. Write *32 – 15* on chart paper. Incorrectly subtract bottom to top in the ones column and top to bottom in the tens columns for a difference of 23. Ask, "How can I check if my answer is correct?"
2. Review the use of addition to check subtraction. Write *23 + 15* on chart paper and find the sum of 38. Point out that 38 and 32 are not the same, so the difference is wrong.
3. Build a base ten model of each number. Ask, "What can I do to make subtracting in the ones column work?" Remind students that borrowing a rod from the tens place and exchanging it for 10 units does not change the value of the number. Count the total number of base ten blocks after borrowing to verify the number is still 32.
4. Subtract in each column. Practice building and subtracting numbers using base ten blocks.
5. Have students describe in their math journals how to solve 41 – 28.

Group 2 □

Checking the Difference
1. Write *54 – 26* on chart paper. Say, "I'm going to subtract, but I'm going to make a mistake. See if you can find my error."
2. Demonstrate subtracting bottom to top in the ones column to get a difference of 32. Ask, "Does it matter in which direction I subtract? How can I check whether this difference is correct? Where did I make a mistake?"
3. Ask a volunteer to demonstrate subtracting from top to bottom, borrowing from the tens place for the ones column. Have all of the students check the difference using inverse operations.
4. Write subtraction problems with regrouping for students to solve. Have students write and solve inverse addition problems to check their answers.
5. Have students write in their math journals about subtraction with regrouping.

Group 3 △

Inverse Operations
1. Write ____ – 48 = 39 on chart paper. Ask, "Would you use subtraction or addition to solve this problem? How can you use addition when the symbol calls for subtraction?" Have students rewrite the problem as an addition problem to solve for the missing number.
2. Remind students that addition and subtraction are inverse operations. Have students describe the parts of the problem using appropriate terminology in both the addition and subtraction version of the problem. (The difference and the subtrahend in the subtraction problem can be written as the addends in the addition problem. The sum of the addition problem is the missing minuend.)
3. Provide a variety of addition and subtraction problems. Let students practice writing and describing the inverse problems.
4. Have students write in their math journals about the relationship between addition and subtraction.

Name_____

Write the subtraction sentence for each model. Then, find each difference.

1.

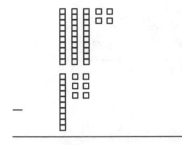

–_____   –_____

2.

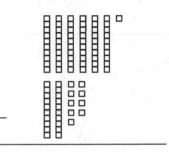

–_____   –_____

Find each difference. Cross off the answer in the bank below.

Answer Bank		
39	27	16
28	14	23

3.   35
   – 7

4.   26
   – 12

5.   48
   – 21

6.   57
   – 18

7.   79
   – 56

8.   63
   – 47

Name_____

Find each difference. Write and solve an inverse addition problem for each subtraction problem to check your work.

1.   42
   − 27

2.   94
   − 36

3.   85
   − 19

4.   29
   − 18

5.   73
   − 57

6.   51
   − 38

7.   261
   − 139

8.   537
   − 228

9.   729
   − 437

10.   612
   − 183

11.   94
   − 56

12.   80
   − 21

Name_____

Use inverse operations to write the missing number in each problem.

1. □
    − 38
    ‾‾‾‾
    43

2. □
    − 17
    ‾‾‾‾
    35

3. 281
    + □
    ‾‾‾‾
    460

4. □
    − 49
    ‾‾‾‾
    15

5. □
    + 352
    ‾‾‾‾
    800

6. □
    − 24
    ‾‾‾‾
    49

7. □
    − 36
    ‾‾‾‾
    54

8. □
    − 29
    ‾‾‾‾
    56

9. 569
    + □
    ‾‾‾‾
    856

10. □
    − 261
    ‾‾‾‾
    715

11. □
    − 138
    ‾‾‾‾
    162

12. 459
    + □
    ‾‾‾‾
    600

 # Number and Operations ·······

Objective
Develop readiness for multiplication by using repeated addition.

Materials:
- Unit cubes or counters
- Grid paper
- Activity sheets (pages 23–25)
- Math journals

Mini-Lesson

1. Gather 6 sets of 2 unit cubes. Ask, "How many pairs of cubes are there?" Refer to one of the pairs as a *set*. Ask, "How many cubes are in each set? How many sets are there?" (There are 6 equal sets of 2.)
2. Ask, "What could I do to find the total number of cubes? How can I write that as an addition sentence?" Write $2 + 2 + 2 + 2 + 2 + 2 = 12$ on the board. Explain that sometimes the number of objects in a set is quite large or you have many sets, so adding to find the total can take too long.
3. Define *multiplication* as a quicker way to add many sets of the same size. Remind students that the model shows 6 equal sets of 2. Write the multiplication sentence $6 \times 2 = 12$. Read the sentence as "6 sets times 2 cubes in each set equals 12 total cubes" or "6 sets of 2 equals 12."
4. Repeat the procedure with 3 sets of 5 unit cubes. Guide students to the addition $(5 + 5 + 5)$ and multiplication (3×5) sentences shown by the model.

Group 1 ◯

Relate Addition and Multiplication
1. Organize unit cubes into 5 sets of 4. Ask, "How many sets are there? How many cubes are in one set? Do all of the sets have the same number of cubes?"
2. Ask students how they could find the total number of cubes using addition. Help them write $4 + 4 + 4 + 4 + 4 = 20$ on chart paper. Point out that there are 4 cubes in each set and 5 equal sets. So, they need to add 5 sets of 4 to find the total number.
3. Group the cubes in different amounts. Have students point to each set as they say, for example, "3 plus 3 plus 3 plus 3" to write a repeated addition sentence. Show students how to count the cubes in the first set and say "3 times," then count the number of sets and say "1, 2, 3, 4" to write a multiplication sentence.
4. Have students write in their math journals about how multiplication is related to addition.

Group 2 ▢

Focus on Sets
1. Use unit cubes to build equal sets. Show students 4 sets of 7 cubes. Ask, "How many cubes are in each set? How many sets do you have? What two numbers would you write in the multiplication sentence?"
2. Have students count by 7s as they point to each set to find the total number of cubes. Ask a volunteer to write the multiplication sentence $4 \times 7 = 28$. Read the sentence as "4 sets of 7 equals 28." Tell students that the multiplication sign is another way of saying "sets of."
3. Arrange the cubes into different groups. Continue saying "sets of" to emphasize the equal groupings. Have students write the multiplication sentence for each arrangement.
4. Challenge students to arrange the same number of cubes in different numbers of sets. Ask, "How does the number of cubes in each set change? Is the total still the same?"
5. Have students write in their math journals about equal sets and how they relate to multiplication problems.

Group 3 △

Multiplication Arrays
1. Distribute grid paper to students. Introduce the term *array* as a group of items arranged in rows and columns. On the grid paper, color 3 rows of 7 units. Ask, "How many rows are colored? Is there an equal number of squares in each row?"
2. Ask, "How many squares are colored altogether? How can I write this array as a repeated addition sentence? How can I write it as a multiplication sentence?" Read the problem as "3 sets of 7 equals 21."
3. Arrange students in pairs and give each pair 32 cubes. Challenge them to arrange the cubes in arrays. Remind students that there must be an equal number of cubes in each row and column. Have them write a multiplication problem for each array.
4. Have students record their arrays on grid paper and label each array with the corresponding multiplication sentence.
5. Have students write in their math journals about using arrays to multiply.

Name_____

Look at each addition sentence. Write the letter of the matching multiplication sentence. Then, find the solution.

1. 6 + 6 + 6 + 6 + 6 _____

2. 9 + 9 + 9 _____

3. 5 + 5 + 5 + 5 _____

4. 8 + 8 + 8 _____

5. 7 + 7 _____

6. 9 + 9 + 9 + 9 + 9 _____

7. 4 + 4 + 4 + 4 _____

8. 3 + 3 + 3 + 3 + 3 + 3 + 3 _____

9. 2 + 2 + 2 + 2 + 2 _____

10. 3 + 3 + 3 + 3 _____

11. 8 + 8 + 8 + 8 + 8 _____

12. 9 + 9 _____

A. $4 \times 5 =$ _____

B. $5 \times 2 =$ _____

C. $5 \times 9 =$ _____

D. $3 \times 8 =$ _____

E. $3 \times 9 =$ _____

F. $4 \times 3 =$ _____

G. $2 \times 7 =$ _____

H. $5 \times 6 =$ _____

I. $5 \times 8 =$ _____

J. $4 \times 4 =$ _____

K. $2 \times 9 =$ _____

L. $7 \times 3 =$ _____

Name_____

Look at each picture. Write the equal sets. Then, write the multiplication sentence.

1.

___ sets of ___

___ × ___ = ___

2.

___ sets of ___

___ × ___ = ___

3.

___ sets of ___

___ × ___ = ___

4.

___ sets of ___

___ × ___ = ___

5.

___ sets of ___

___ × ___ = ___

6.

___ sets of ___

___ × ___ = ___

7.

___ sets of ___

___ × ___ = ___

8.

___ sets of ___

___ × ___ = ___

Name_____

Look at each array. Write the repeated addition sentence. Then, write the multiplication sentence.

1.

___ + ___ + ___ + ___ = ___

___ × ___ = ___

2. ○○○○○○○○
○○○○○○○○

___ + ___ = ___

___ × ___ = ___

3. △△△△△
△△△△△
△△△△△

___ + ___ + ___ = ___

___ × ___ = ___

4. ☆☆☆☆☆☆☆
☆☆☆☆☆☆☆

___ + ___ = ___

___ × ___ = ___

5. ○○○○○○○○
○○○○○○○○
○○○○○○○○

___ + ___ + ___ = ___

___ × ___ = ___

6. △△△
△△△
△△△
△△△

___ + ___ + ___ + ___ = ___

___ × ___ = ___

7. ⬡⬡⬡⬡⬡⬡
⬡⬡⬡⬡⬡

___ + ___ = ___

___ × ___ = ___

8. ☾☾☾☾☾☾☾
☾☾☾☾☾☾☾
☾☾☾☾☾☾☾

___ + ___ + ___ = ___

___ × ___ = ___

Number and Operations

Objective
Skip count by 2s.

Mini-Lesson

1. Define *skip counting* as counting in groups, like 2s, 5s, or 10s.
2. Distribute two counters to each student. Ask a small group of students to stand. Have a volunteer count the total number of counters using skip counting. Repeat with several groupings.
3. Place a pile of 30 counters on the table. Divide the pile into equal groups of two counters. Ask, "Is the total number of counters even or odd? How do you know?" Repeat with 19 counters. Define an *even* number as one that can be split evenly into two groups. There is not a counter left, so when skip counting by even numbers, you start at zero. When an odd number is split into two equal groups, there is always one left over. When skip counting by odd numbers, start at one. Use a number line to illustrate how even and odd numbers skip count by 2s.
4. Start at 0 and skip count to 40. Ask, "What do you notice about even numbers?" Point to the pattern in the ones place. Start at 1 and do the same with odd numbers. Ask, "Do the groups share any common numbers? Why not?"
5. Practice skip counting forward and backward by 2s starting at different numbers. Use a number line or hundreds chart as a visual reference.

Group 1 ○

Reinforce Pattern
1. Review the terms *even* and *odd*. Give examples of each. Reinforce the concept of skip counting as counting in groups. This will build the foundation for multiples later.
2. Start at 2. Mark all of the even numbers on a number line with the same color counter. Say them aloud together as you point to each one. Ask, "What numbers are skipped? Why?"
3. Leave the even counters. Start at 1 and mark odd numbers with counters on the opposite color side. Say them aloud together as you point to each one.
4. Ask, "How can you tell whether a number is even or odd?" Discuss the pattern of numbers in the ones place for both kinds of numbers. Write several numbers on chart paper. Ask students to classify each number as even or odd based on the digit in the ones place.
5. Ask students to list examples of even and odd numbers in their math journals.

Group 2 □

Practice Skip Counting
1. Use a hundreds chart and counters as a visual reference of odds and evens. Give each student crayons and a copy of a hundreds chart. Have students start at 2 and color all of the even numbers on their charts. Ask, "What is an even number? How can you tell if a number is even?" Repeat with odd numbers using a different color.
2. Ask, "What digits are in the ones place in even numbers? Odd numbers? Is that always true, even for very large numbers? Why?"
3. Start on the number 24. Then, give directions for skip counting. For example, skip count by 2s backward from 24 five times. Ask, "What is the number?" Follow the same process with other even and odd numbers, giving directions to skip count forward and backward.
4. Have students write skip counting riddles in their math journals. Let students share their riddles with each other to solve.

Group 3 △

Identify Multiples of 2
1. Brainstorm everyday objects that come in pairs. Discuss the ease of counting a large quantity of any of these things using multiples of 2. Ask questions like, "How many socks are 5 people wearing? How many eyes are watching a show with 12 audience members?" Have students skip count by 2s to determine the answers.
2. Challenge students to give examples of very large numbers that are multiples of 2. Reinforce the pattern of looking at the ones place to determine if a number is even or odd.
3. Discuss multiples of other numbers, such as 10, 5, and 3. Use a hundreds chart to mark the multiples and investigate where numbers overlap categories.
4. Have students write in their math journals to answer the question: If you can skip count by 2 along odd numbers, why are odd numbers not multiples of 2?

Name_____

Start at 16. Color the path of circles as you skip count by 2s.

16	18	19	21	23
17	20	22	24	35
15	29	27	26	30
23	32	28	25	32
34	30	39	37	30
36	38	40	42	44

Name_____

Start with the first number in each row. Skip count by 2s. Write the numbers in order on the lines. Then, tell whether the numbers are even or odd.

Skip Count   Even or Odd

I. 48 _____ _____ _____ _____   _____

2. 35 _____ _____ _____ _____   _____

3. 20 _____ _____ _____ _____   _____

4. 73 _____ _____ _____ _____   _____

5. 64 _____ _____ _____ _____   _____

6. 9 _____ _____ _____ _____   _____

7. 81 _____ _____ _____ _____   _____

8. 92 _____ _____ _____ _____   _____

Skip count by 2s to follow the directions.

9. Counting forward, write all of the odd numbers between 18 and 31.

_____

10. Counting backward, write all of the even numbers between 109 and 95.

_____

11. Counting backward, write all of the odd numbers between 60 and 49.

_____

12. Counting forward, write all of the even numbers between 43 and 57.

_____

Name_____

Each list skip counts by 2s. Circle the number in each list that is NOT correct. Write the correct number. Then, write *yes* or *no* to show if the numbers are multiples of 2.

	Correct Number	Multiple of 2
1. 86, 85, 82, 80, 78, 76, 74, 72	_____	_____
2. 19, 21, 23, 25, 28, 29, 31, 33	_____	_____
3. 42, 44, 46, 48, 51, 52, 54, 56	_____	_____
4. 103, 101, 98, 97, 95, 93, 91, 89	_____	_____
5. 58, 60, 62, 63, 66, 68, 70, 72	_____	_____
6. 914, 915, 918, 920, 922, 924, 926	_____	_____

Read each problem. Answer the question. Draw a sketch to show your work.

7. Each car has 2 headlights. There are 7 cars in a parking lot. How many total headlights are there?

8. Allie folds 12 pairs of socks. How many socks are there in all?

9. A store orders 19 pairs of new tennis shoes. How many total shoes are ordered?

Number and Operations

Materials:
- Number line
- Two-color counters
- Copies of a hundreds chart
- Chart paper
- Grid paper
- Crayons
- Activity sheets (pages 31–33)
- Math journals

Objective
Skip count by 5s.

Mini-Lesson

1. Review the term *skip counting*. Look at a hundreds chart together. Start at 5 and skip count by 5s to 100, placing counters as you count aloud. Ask, "What do you notice about these numbers?" Point out that multiples of 5 always have a 0 or 5 in the ones place.
2. Using the hundreds chart, point to a multiple of 5 and model how to skip count forward and backward from this number. Give students a number to start on and have them try on their own.
3. Then, organize unit cubes in sets of 5. Practice skip counting the sets, emphasizing that the final number is the total number of cubes in all of the sets.

Group 1 ○

Practicing Skip Counting

1. Ask, "How many fingers are on each hand? How many toes are on each foot? How could I find the total number of fingers or toes here in the group? What is a quick way to find that sum?" Skip count the total number of fingers together.
2. Review the pattern of digits in the ones place for multiples of 5. Have students color all of the multiples of 5 on a hundreds chart. Ask, "What digits do each of these numbers end in? Does this make it easier to spot them on the chart?"
3. Start from different multiples of 5 and model how to skip count forward and backward from each number. Practice this several times together, then in student pairs.
4. Have students write a list of numbers skip counted by 5 in their math journals.

Group 2 □

Using Skip Counting

1. Brainstorm everyday things that come in fives (fingers, toes, points on a star, etc.). Discuss the benefit of skip counting versus counting each unit of a large set.
2. Gather a pile of nickels. Ask, "How much is each nickel worth? How can you count the total amount of money you have?" Explain that instead of having a big pile of pennies to count, they can skip count the pile of nickels by 5s to know how much money is there. Skip count the money together.
3. Organize unit cubes in sets of 5. Model how to skip count by 5s to add to and subtract from the total amount of cubes.
4. Have students write in their math journals about why skip counting by 5s is useful.

Group 3 △

Identifying Multiples of 5

1. Review the terms *even* and *odd*. Ask, "What numbers do even numbers end in? Odd numbers?" Skip count by 5s and write a list of several of the numbers on chart paper. Explain that these numbers are called *multiples* of five. Ask, "What numbers do multiples of 5 end in? Are multiples of 5 even or odd numbers?" Discuss how some multiples of 5 are even and some are odd.
2. Distribute grid paper to students. Have them color squares in rows of 5 and skip count the total number of squares they colored on their grid paper by 5s. Ask, "How can you write the number of rows of 5 as an addition sentence? As a multiplication sentence?" Explain that the number of rows of 5 are multiples of 5. Ask, "How many rows of 5 would you need to color 45 squares?" Continue with other multiples of 5.
3. Have students write in their math journals to explain how skip counting is related to multiplication.

Name_____

Skip count to find the total number in each group.

1.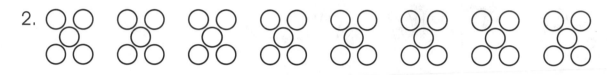

_____triangles

2.

_____circles

3.

_____stars

Skip count by 5s. Write the missing numbers in each list.

4. 25, 30, ___, 40, 45, ___, 55, 60

5. 70, ___, 80, ___, ___, 95, ___, ___, 110

6. 50, 55, ___, ___, ___, 75, ___

7. ___, 140, 145, 150, ___, ___, ___, 170

8. ___, ___, 20, ___, ___, 35, 40, ___, ___

Name_____

Skip count to find the total number in each group.

1.

    _____pieces of pie

2.

    _____fingers

3.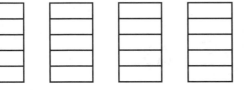

    _____sections

4.

    _____crayons

Skip count forward or backward by 5s from the number given.

5. forward   25, ___, ___, ___, ___

6. backward   90, ___, ___, ___, ___

7. forward   70, ___, ___, ___, ___

8. backward   40, ___, ___, ___, ___

32

Name_____

Write the multiplication problem for each array.

1. ☐☐☐☐☐
☐☐☐☐☐

_____ × _____ = _____

2. ☐☐☐☐☐
☐☐☐☐☐
☐☐☐☐☐

_____ × _____ = _____

3. ☐☐☐☐☐
☐☐☐☐☐
☐☐☐☐☐
☐☐☐☐☐
☐☐☐☐☐
☐☐☐☐☐

_____ × _____ = _____

4. ☐☐☐☐☐
☐☐☐☐☐
☐☐☐☐☐
☐☐☐☐☐
☐☐☐☐☐

_____ × _____ = _____

Answer each question below. Draw a sketch to show each problem.

5. A watermelon is cut into 6 slices. Each slice has 5 seeds in it. How many total seeds are in the watermelon? _____

6. A chef bakes 5 pizzas. Each pizza is cut into 5 equal slices. How many total slices of pizza did the chef bake? _____

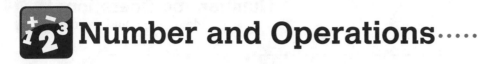

Number and Operations

Materials:
- Unit cubes
- Small plates or bowls
- Counters
- Activity sheets (pages 35–37)

Objective
Develop readiness for division by using repeated subtraction.

Mini-Lesson

1. Define *division* as breaking a whole into equal groups. Use unit cubes to represent a batch of 24 cookies. Say, "I want to divide this batch of 24 cookies evenly among 4 students." Hand four students one unit cube each. Say, "I need equal groups of 4 so that all of the students get the same number of cookies."
2. Write 24 – 4 = 20 on chart paper. Distribute another group of 4 cookies and write another – 4 after the 20. Continue to distribute cookies in groups of 4 until they are gone, writing – 4 each time. Point out that each student has the same number of cookies. Ask, "How many equal groups of 4 did I hand out?" Compare the number of unit cubes in each group to the number of times you subtracted 4 from the total.
3. Use the unit cubes to model how to break the same set of 24 into equal groups of 2, 3, 6, and 8. Relate repeated subtraction to division in each example.

Group 1 ○

Sharing Equally

1. Focus on the phrase *equal groups*. Reiterate that this means all of the groups have the same number in them. Emphasize that division means to break apart a whole into equal groups.
2. Place 12 counters on a table with 3 plates or bowls. Tell students to share the counters between 3 equal groups. Model how to take 3 of the counters from the group of 12 and place one in each plate. Have volunteers help sort the rest into the plates in the same manner. Count how many counters are in each plate.
3. Write a subtraction sentence that shows the equal groups. Write *12 – 3 – 3 – 3 – 3 = 0*. Explain that there were 12 counters, and you shared 3 at a time until there were 0 left. Relate the number of subtracted 3s to the number of counters in each bowl.
4. Repeat the steps, dividing 8 counters into 4 equal groups, 15 counters into 5 equal groups, and 18 counters into 3 equal groups.

Group 2 □

Subtracting Groups

1. Remind students that division means breaking a whole into equal groups. Ask, "How can I divide this group of 18 counters into 2 equal groups?" Have a volunteer pull counters 2 at a time away from the group, placing each into one of two rows. Continue separating the pile this way, keeping a tally of the number of times 2 counters are pulled from the main group.
2. Ask, "How many counters did we start with?" Write *18*. Ask, "How many counters were pulled away at a time?" Write *– 2*. Ask, "How many times did we pull 2 counters from the group?" Write *–2* eight more times (for a total of 9 times).
3. Ask, "What does the number of times we subtracted 2 from the pile represent?" Explain that the number of tallies (or number of times 2 was subtracted from the pile) equals the number of counters in each group.
4. Write *18 ÷ 2 = 9* on chart paper. Point to the array of counters and explain that the sentence says, "18 counters divided into 2 equal groups equals 9 counters in each group."

Group 3 △

Creating Arrays

1. Arrange 24 counters into a 6 x 4 array. Ask, "How does this array represent a multiplication sentence?" Have a volunteer point out the 6 equal rows of 4. Ask, "Is there another multiplication sentence that could be represented by this array?" Write *4 × 6 = 24* and *6 × 4 = 24*.
2. Remind students that addition and subtraction are inverse operations; they undo one another. Multiplication and division work the same way. Ask, "How could this same array represent a division sentence? Is this the only division sentence represented?" Write *24 ÷ 6 = 4* and *24 ÷ 4 = 6* under the multiplication facts.
3. Ask, "What do each of these math sentences have in common?" Define *fact families* as a related group of math sentences that use inverse operations to get other members of the same family.
4. Challenge students to use the manipulatives to create arrays and write the members of each fact family represented by the model.

Name_____

Draw circles around equal groups to show how the total can be shared by the number of people shown.

1. 4 people

2. 3 people

3. 5 people

4. 2 people

5. 3 people

6. 4 people

7. 6 people

8. 5 people

Name_____

Draw the marbles divided equally on the plates. Then, write the subtraction and division sentences.

1. 24 marbles

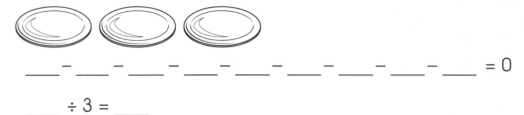

___ - ___ - ___ - ___ - ___ - ___ - ___ - ___ - ___ = 0

___ ÷ 3 = ___

2. 20 marbles

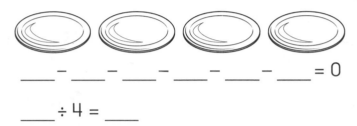

___ - ___ - ___ - ___ - ___ - ___ = 0

___ ÷ 4 = ___

3. 18 marbles

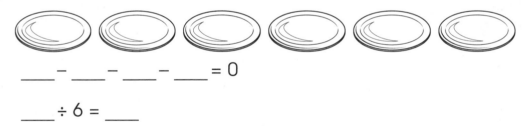

___ - ___ - ___ - ___ = 0

___ ÷ 6 = ___

4. 21 marbles

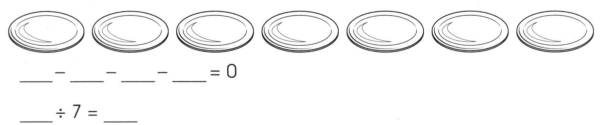

___ - ___ - ___ - ___ = 0

___ ÷ 7 = ___

5. 32 marbles

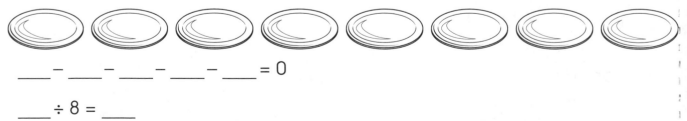

___ - ___ - ___ - ___ - ___ = 0

___ ÷ 8 = ___

Name_____

Sketch an array to help solve each division sentence. Write the other members of each fact family.

1. 12 ÷ 6 = ___

___ ÷ ___ = ___

___ × ___ = ___

___ × ___ = ___

2. 20 ÷ 4 = ___

___ ÷ ___ = ___

___ × ___ = ___

___ × ___ = ___

3. 18 ÷ 3 = ___

___ ÷ ___ = ___

___ × ___ = ___

___ × ___ = ___

4. 24 ÷ 6 = ___

___ ÷ ___ = ___

___ × ___ = ___

___ × ___ = ___

5. 36 ÷ 9 = ___

___ ÷ ___ = ___

___ × ___ = ___

___ × ___ = ___

6. 14 ÷ 2 = ___

___ ÷ ___ = ___

___ × ___ = ___

___ × ___ = ___

7. 12 ÷ 3 = ___

___ ÷ ___ = ___

___ × ___ = ___

___ × ___ = ___

8. 28 ÷ 4 = ___

___ ÷ ___ = ___

___ × ___ = ___

___ × ___ = ___

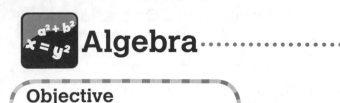

Algebra

Materials:
- Pattern blocks
- Counters of different colors
- Chart paper
- Activity sheets (pages 39–41)
- Math journals

Objective
Identify and extend shape patterns.

Mini-Lesson

1. Lay a pattern of multicolored counters in a row on a table. Ask, "How are these counters alike?" Discuss how the counters are the same size and shape. Ask, "How are the counters different?" Define the term *pattern*.
2. Give each student a handful of counters. Have them arrange their counters in a pattern you create. Model how to say the pattern aloud.
3. Invite a volunteer to extend the pattern for the group. Have students extend this pattern with their counters.
4. Follow the same procedure with pattern blocks. Focus on saying the pattern aloud to identify the part that repeats.
5. Have student pairs practice making and extending patterns with the tangrams. Ask volunteers to model some pattern examples and explain how to extend the patterns. Encourage the use of correct math vocabulary.

Group 1 ○

Reinforce Repetition

1. Draw a pattern of alternating stars and circles. Ask the group to name the shapes aloud. Ask, "What is the part that repeats?" Identify this as the pattern. Say the pattern aloud in rhythm. Model how to extend this pattern.
2. Use pattern blocks to create a pattern. Repeat the pattern a few times so that students can identify the repeating part. Together, name the shapes aloud rhythmically, pausing between each set of four shapes to help students identify the pattern.
3. Use pattern blocks to create a repeating trio. (For example, trapezoid, triangle, rhombus.) Ask, "How many shapes are in the repeating part of the pattern? How many times does this whole group repeat? What shapes come next in order?" Have a volunteer use pattern blocks to extend the pattern.
4. Invite a student to create a pattern using pattern blocks. Have the group identify and extend the pattern. Say the shape names aloud to reinforce the rhythm of the pattern.

Group 2 □

Name Shape Patterns

1. Draw a pattern of repeating shapes. (For example, circle, circle, triangle.) Ask students to name the shapes aloud. Ask, "Which section of shapes repeats?" Identify this as the pattern.
2. Ask, "How can we name this shape pattern using letters to match the pattern?" The first two shapes are the same, the third is different. Write *AAB* on chart paper. With students, say the letter pattern aloud rhythmically as you point to each shape in the pattern.
3. Use pattern blocks to create another pattern. Repeat the pattern a few times. Ask a volunteer to name the shapes aloud and challenge the group to identify the pattern and name it using letters. Let a volunteer extend the pattern using the pattern blocks.
4. Let students create their own patterns with pattern blocks. Challenge them to identify, name, and extend their patterns. Have students record their patterns in their math journals.

Group 3 △

Translated Shape Patterns

1. Use identical pattern blocks to create a pattern of translated shapes. (For example, eight trapezoids, each showing the shape turned 90° so that the pattern repeats twice.) Ask volunteers to identify and describe the pattern. Use identical pattern blocks to extend the shape pattern.
2. Follow the same procedure with letters. Write a repeating pattern of mirror image capital B's on chart paper. Ask students to identify the repeating portion and continue the pattern.
3. Invite students to create their own patterns. Give each student a pattern block and have her trace the shape, turning or reflecting the shape to create each different element of the pattern.
4. Have students write in their math journals about how to use just one shape to create an ABCA shape pattern.

Name_____

Circle the part that repeats in each pattern.

1. ▯⬡▯⬡▯⬡▯⬡

2. ☆☆☆△☆☆☆△☆☆☆△

3. ▢◇⇨▢◇⇨▢◇⇨

4. ⏢△○○▢△⏢△○○▢⏢△○○▢

5. ⬡○△⬡○△⬡○△⬡○△

Draw the part that repeats in each pattern.

6. ☆▢☆▢☆▢

7.

8. ▯△▢▯△△▯△▯

Name_____

Above each shape pattern, write the matching letter pattern from the bank below.

Letter Pattern Bank				
AB	ABCC	ABBA	AABC	ABAC
AAB	ABC	AAAB	ABBB	ABCD

1. _____

2. _____

3. _____

4. _____

5. _____

6. _____

7. _____

8. _____

9. _____

10. _____

40

Name_____

Draw the next figure in each pattern.

1.

2.

3.

4.

5.

6.

7.

8.

9.

10.

 **Algebra**

Objective
Identify and extend number patterns.

Materials:
- Number line
- Chart paper
- Yardstick
- Counters
- Activity sheets (pages 43–45)

Mini-Lesson

1. Write the following list of numbers on chart paper: *4, 7, 10, 13, 16, 19*. Have students mark each number on a number line with a counter. Ask, "Do the numbers get larger or smaller? Do they change by the same amount each time?"
2. Model how to find the difference between the first pair of numbers in the list. Then, check the difference between each consecutive pair. Tell students that the numbers in the list get larger by 3. Demonstrate how to extend the pattern by writing the next several numbers.
3. Use the same questions from the first step with *22, 20, 18, 16*, and *14*. Reinforce that moving to the left on a number line means subtraction (getting smaller), and moving to the right means addition (getting larger).
4. Discuss the number pattern together. Have students use counters on the number line to find the next three numbers.

Group 1 ○

Practice Number Patterns

1. Ask, "What is a *pattern*? Do patterns have to use pictures? What number patterns do you know?" Give examples of numbers that increase or decrease in patterns (2s, 5s, 10s, 100s).
2. Write the following numbers on chart paper: *9, 11, 13, 15, 17*. Tell students to find each number on a number line in order and mark with counters.
3. Ask, "Do the numbers get larger or smaller? Do they change by the same amount each time? What is the pattern?"
4. Study the counters on the number line together. Model how to continue the pattern by adding 2 to each number. Have students place a counter on each new number in the pattern.
5. Repeat this process with a subtraction number pattern. (For example, 24, 21, 18, 15, 12.) Discuss the previous questions and have students extend the pattern to 0. Use the number line to emphasize the concept of addition (moving to the right) and subtraction (moving to the left).

Group 2 □

Identify Number Patterns

1. Discuss patterns in everyday life. Ask, "Can you think of number patterns in your everyday life?" (For example, days in a week, months in a year, years in a decade, minutes in an hour, hours in a day, numerals on a clock, inches in a foot, feet in a mile.) Identify the repeating pattern in each example.
2. Write the following numbers on the board: *15, 22, 29, 36, 43, 50*. Ask, "Are the numbers getting larger or smaller by the same amount each time? What is the pattern for this group of numbers? What would be the next number in the pattern?" Follow the same process for a subtraction sequence.
3. Write the following numbers on the board: *2, 7, 9, 10, 13, 17*. Ask, "Are the numbers getting larger or smaller? Do they change by the same amount each time? Is there a way to predict what number will come next? Is there a pattern here?"
4. Have students write in their math journals to explain how to identify a number pattern.

Group 3 △

Grow Number Patterns

1. Challenge students with an example of a pattern that changes by a different amount each time, but in a predictable way. For example, 1, 2, 4, 7, 11, 16, 22 (+1, +2, +3, +4, +5, +6) or 90, 85, 75, 60 (−5, −10, −15). Discuss together how to find the difference between consecutive numbers. Ask, "How do the numbers change each time?"
2. Explain that the difference between each pair of consecutive numbers is a pattern in itself. Ask, "What is the pattern for creating this group of numbers? How can we extend the pattern?" Follow the same process for a subtraction sequence.
3. Invite students to create their own growing patterns. Emphasize that the pattern has to be consistent so that it is recognizable. Have students identify and extend each number pattern example.
4. Have students write in their math journals about the importance of consistency in identifying a pattern in a list of numbers.

Name_____

Use the number line below. Write the next three numbers in each pattern.

1. 3, 6, 9, 12, 15, _____, _____, _____

2. 1, 5, 9, 13, 17, _____, _____, _____

3. 17, 15, 13, 11, 9, _____, _____, _____

4. 45, 40, 35, 30, 25, _____, _____, _____

5. 8, 10, 12, 14, 16, _____, _____, _____

6. 2, 8, 14, 20, 26, _____, _____, _____

7. 33, 29, 25, 21, 17, _____, _____, _____

8. 6, 11, 16, 21, 26, _____, _____, _____

9. 28, 25, 22, 19, 16, _____, _____, _____

10. 45, 39, 33, 27, 21, _____, _____, _____

Name_____

Identify the pattern in each series of numbers. Write the next number in the pattern.

1. 21, 23, 25, 27, 29, _____   Pattern: _____

2. 36, 33, 30, 27, 24, _____   Pattern: _____

3. 1, 7, 13, 19, 25, _____   Pattern: _____

4. 42, 38, 34, 30, 26, _____   Pattern: _____

5. 3, 8, 13, 18, 23, _____   Pattern: _____

6. 24, 34, 44, 54, 64, _____   Pattern: _____

7. 64, 56, 48, 40, 32, _____   Pattern: _____

8. 91, 82, 73, 64, 55, _____   Pattern: _____

9. 13, 25, 37, 49, 61, _____   Pattern: _____

10. 101, 86, 71, 56, _____   Pattern: _____

11. 82, 75, 68, 61, 54, _____   Pattern: _____

12. 17, 40, 63, 86, 109, _____   Pattern: _____

Name_____

Write the missing numbers in each pattern.

1. 33, 37, _____, 45, 49, 53, _____, _____

2. _____, 24, 22, _____, 18, 16, 14, _____

3. 11, 20, 29, 38, _____, 56, _____, _____

4. 36, _____, 56, 66, 76, _____, _____, 106

5. 97, 94, 91, _____, 85, 82, _____, _____

6. _____, _____, _____, 32, 26, 20, 14

7. 15, _____, 31, 39, 47, _____, _____, 71

Find each pattern. Write the next three numbers.

8. 2, 4, 8, 14, 22, _____, _____, _____

9. 52, 51, 48, 43, 36, _____, _____, _____

10. 200, 195, 185, 170, 150, _____, _____, _____

11. 1, 4, 10, 19, 31, 46, _____, _____, _____

12. 23, 24, 26, 29, 33, _____, _____, _____

 **Algebra**

Materials:
- Hundreds charts
- Counters
- Chart paper
- Activity sheets (pages 47–49)
- Math journals

Objective

Write the rules for given patterns.

Mini-Lesson

1. Ask, "What is a *rule*? What are some rules you follow?" Explain that numbers also follow rules. A group of numbers can be organized by a rule, or consistent pattern. Write the words *add* and *subtract* and their symbols.
2. Give each student a hundreds chart. Write the following list on chart paper: *7, 11, 15, 19, 23, 27*. Have students mark each number on the hundreds chart in order with a counter. Ask, "Do the numbers get larger or smaller? Is this an addition or subtraction rule?"
3. Model how to find the difference between the first pair of numbers in the list. Use words to describe the rule (add four). Check that the pattern is consistent between each consecutive pair of numbers in the list. Determine the rule for the entire pattern.
4. Follow the same process for *18, 15, 12, 9, 6, 3*. Discuss the number pattern. Determine the rule for the list together. Write the rule in words.

Group 1 ○

Review Vocabulary

1. Define the terms *rule, add,* and *subtract*. Emphasize that number patterns that follow a rule change by the same amount each time.
2. Use counters to display a number pattern. Place 2 counters in one pile, 4 counters in the next pile, and increase the number of counters by 2 in the next several groups. Ask students to identify the number of counters in each group.
3. Ask, "Are the numbers getting larger or smaller? Do you add or subtract counters to get to the next group? What is the rule for this pattern?" Write *Rule: add two counters* and point to each word when you say the rule aloud.
4. Regroup the counters in a new pattern. (For example, 6, 5, 4, 3, 2.) Study and count the number of counters in each pile. Ask the same questions and write the rule together.
5. Write the lesson vocabulary terms on chart paper. Have students write in their math journals about pattern rules.

Group 2 ▢

Identify Pattern Rules

1. Discuss everyday examples of number pattern rules. Consider pairs of shoes. There are 2 shoes in one pair, 4 shoes in two pairs, 6 shoes in three pairs, etc. Challenge students to generate a list of addition number patterns in everyday life (number of insect legs in a consecutive number of insects, wheels on cars, tires on tricycles, cartons of a dozen eggs). Identify the rule for each list.
2. Follow the same process for subtraction rules (selling sets of marbles, a dog eating two pounds of food at each meal, planting four seeds in each row of a garden). Discuss and write the rule for each situation in words.
3. Challenge each student pair to write a list of numbers that follows a rule. Allow each pair to present their list, and have the rest of the group identify and describe the rule.
4. Have students write in their math journals about pattern rules. Encourage them to use lesson vocabulary and an example in their writing.

Group 3 △

Apply Rules

1. Remind students that numbers in a pattern change by the same amount each time. Ask, "How can you tell if a list of numbers has an addition or subtraction rule?"
2. Say the following list aloud: 17, 20, 23, 26, 29. Have students place a counter on each number in order on a hundreds chart. Ask, "How are the numbers changing? Is this an addition or subtraction rule? What is the rule for this pattern?" Write *+ 3* and check if it works for each consecutive pair of numbers in the list. Then, apply the rule to extend the list. Follow the same steps with a subtraction number pattern.
3. Write the rule *+ 5*. Have students start on a number they choose and place counters on every number that follows the rule. Have students share their lists for the rule. Ask, "Is the rule the same for all of our patterns? Are all of our patterns the same? Why is this?"
4. Have students explain in their math journals how to find the rule for a number pattern.

Name_____

Describe each pattern's rule. The first one is done for you.

1.

   Add one balloon. _____

2.

   _____

3.

   _____

4.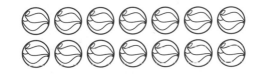

   _____

5.

   _____

6.

   _____

Name_____

Look at each pattern. Write each rule on the line.

1. 1, 4, 7, 10, 13, 16   Rule:_____

2. 30, 26, 22, 18, 14, 10   Rule:_____

3. 45, 40, 35, 30, 25, 20   Rule:_____

4. 11, 13, 15, 17, 19, 21   Rule:_____

5. 6, 13, 20, 27, 34, 41   Rule:_____

6. 48, 42, 36, 30, 24, 18   Rule:_____

Read the rule. Circle the pattern that follows the rule.

7. Rule: add 4

   2, 5, 8, 11, 14, 17

   3, 7, 11, 15, 19, 23

   1, 6, 11, 16, 21, 26

8. Rule: subtract 3

   28, 26, 24, 22, 20, 18

   22, 25, 28, 31, 34, 37

   27, 24, 21, 18, 15, 12

9. Rule: subtract 9

   71, 62, 53, 44, 35, 26

   63, 53, 43, 33, 23, 13

   80, 69, 58, 47, 36, 25

10. Rule: add 6

   14, 21, 28, 35, 42, 49

   15, 21, 27, 33, 39, 45

   16, 23, 30, 37, 44, 51

11. Rule: add 5

   42, 37, 32, 27, 22, 17

   19, 24, 29, 34, 39, 44

   18, 24, 30, 36, 42, 48

12. Rule: subtract 7

   64, 55, 46, 37, 28, 19

   58, 50, 42, 36, 28, 20

   61, 54, 47, 40, 33, 26

48

Name_____

Write the rule for each pattern.

1. 60, 56, 52, 48, 44, 40

   Rule: _____

2. 23, 29, 35, 41, 47, 53

   Rule: _____

3. 87, 82, 77, 72, 67, 62

   Rule: _____

4. 58, 61, 64, 67, 70, 73

   Rule: _____

5. 34, 44, 54, 64, 74, 84

   Rule: _____

Write a pattern of six numbers for each rule below.

6. Rule: + 8 _____, _____, _____, _____, _____, _____

7. Rule: – 9 _____, _____, _____, _____, _____, _____

8. Rule: – 12 _____, _____, _____, _____, _____, _____

9. Rule: + 7 _____, _____, _____, _____, _____, _____

10. Rule: – 11 _____, _____, _____, _____, _____, _____

11. Rule: – 6 _____, _____, _____, _____, _____, _____

12. Rule: + 13 _____, _____, _____, _____, _____, _____

 **Algebra** ·········· · · · · · · · · · · ·

Materials:
- Chart paper
- Colorful markers
- Index cards
- Cubes
- Cups
- Grid paper
- Activity sheets (pages 51–53)
- Math journals

Objective
Model problem situations using objects, numbers, and other symbols.

Mini-Lesson

1. On chart paper, draw three squares with one colorful marker and four squares with a different colorful marker. Ask, "What does this model show? How many of each color square do you see? What would this model look like using numbers?" Write *3 + 4* under the squares.
2. Ask, "How can you find the answer to this problem? Will the answer be larger or smaller than the numbers in the problem?" Reinforce that addition and multiplication brings groups together, while subtraction and division separate groups. Write the sum to complete the sentence.
3. Draw 10 circles and draw a large X over 3 of the circles. Ask, "What is this model showing—bringing groups together or separating them? What do the X's mean? What kind of problem does this model show?" Write *10 – 3 = 7* and discuss how each number is expressed in the model.

Group 1 ◯

Connect Models and Expressions

1. Draw 12 bananas and 7 apples on chart paper. Ask, "I want to find the total number of fruits. What kind of problem is this? How can I show it using numbers?"
2. Count the number of bananas and write the total under that fruit. Do the same for the apples. Ask, "Does the word *total* mean addition or subtraction? Which symbol should I use between the numbers?" Write *12 + 7* and find the total by counting all of the fruit.
3. Ask, "How many bananas do I have? If I eat 3 bananas on the way home from the store, how can I show that in my model? (Cross off 3 bananas.) How can I find the total number of bananas I have now? What would that look like in numbers?" Write *12 – 3* and demonstrate how to find the difference.
4. Write addition and subtraction expressions on index cards. Let students choose expressions and draw the matching models to solve in their math journals.

Group 2 ▢

Math Sentences

1. Tell students they can use pictures, objects, models, or drawings to help them solve problems. Sometimes, seeing a problem in a different way can make the answer easier to find.
2. On chart paper, draw 6 shaded circles and 8 unshaded circles. Ask, "What does this model show? What would this model look like using numbers?" Write *6 + 8 = 14* under the problem. Have students verify the answer by counting the circles.
3. Draw a set of 14 circles. Draw a large X over 6 of the circles. Ask, "What kind of problem does this model show? What do the X's mean? What does this look like as a number sentence?" Write *14 – 6 = 8* on the paper. Have students verify the answer using the model.
4. Look at the 6 shaded circles and 8 unshaded circles again. Ask, "How could you see this as a subtraction problem? How many more circles are unshaded than shaded?" Write *8 – 6 = 2*.
5. Have students draw models in their math journals and write the matching math sentences.

Group 3 △

Model Multiple Equations

1. Place an array of two different colors of cubes on a table. (For example, 7 red and 13 blue arranged in 4 rows of 5.) Ask, "What equation does this model show?" Accept all suggestions that are mathematically sound. For example, red cubes plus blue cubes, blue cubes minus red cubes, division of the total number of cubes by 5 or 4, or multiplication of 4 rows of 5 cubes.
2. Write all of the equations and discuss how they each represent the model.
3. Let students experiment with unit cubes. Provide empty cups for grouping, take-away, or division. Have students write various equations for the models.
4. Have students draw sketches of their models and corresponding equations in their math journals.

Name_____

Match each model to the correct equation. Use the model to solve.

1. 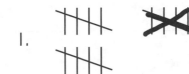 _____   a. 5 + 3 = _____

2.  _____   b. 24 − 8 = _____

3.  _____   c. 6 + 5 = _____

4.  _____   d. 8 + 8 = _____

5. _____   e. 15 − 5 = _____

6. 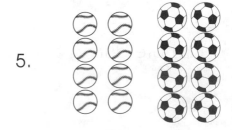 _____   f. 9 − 4 = _____

Name_____

Write and solve a math equation for each model.

1. ⊗⊗⊗⊗⊗⊗⊗⊗○○○○○○ _____

2. ■■■■■■□□□□□ _____

3. ⊠⊠⊠⊠△△△△△△△△ _____

4. ☆☆☆☆★★★★★★★★ _____

5. ⬠⬠⬠⬠⬠⬠⬠⬠⬠⬠ _____

Write and solve a math equation for each problem. Draw a picture to find the answer.

6. Marcus had 17 trading cards. He gave 9 to his little brother. How many trading cards does Marcus have left?

7. A waitress made 15 side salads during lunch and 12 more during dinner. How many side salads did she make in all?

8. Nicole had 14 sunflowers to plant. She planted 8 of the flowers. How many more sunflowers does she have left to plant?

52

Name_____

Look at each model. Write and solve two equations each model could represent. Use different operations in each pair of equations.

1.

_____

2.

_____

3.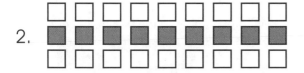

_____

4.

_____

Write and solve an equation for each problem.

5. There are 28 student desks in a classroom. The teacher wants to put the desks into 4 equal rows. How many desks will go in each row?

_____

6. Ben raked and filled 8 bags of leaves. Each bag weighed 10 pounds. How many total pounds of leaves did Ben rake?

_____

 **Algebra**

Materials:
- Index cards
- Chart paper
- Number line
- Counters
- Activity sheets (pages 55–57)
- Math journals

Objective
Represent an unknown quantity as a variable using a symbol.

Mini-Lesson

1. Define the term *symbol* as a shape that stands for something else. Draw examples of symbols on chart paper like a box, a circle, and a triangle. Write the following math sentence, drawing a box where indicated: $5 + \square = 8$. Explain that the box stands for a number that makes this sentence true. Remind students that for a math sentence to be true, the amount needs to be balanced or equal on both sides.
2. Tell students to look at the operation sign first. Say, "Five plus what number equals eight?" Write 2 in the box. Ask, "Does the number two make this sentence true? Why or why not?" Try other numbers until students find the correct one.
3. Follow the same process for a subtraction sentence: $\square - 2 = 7$. Ask, "Will the number in the box be larger or smaller than the other numbers in the problem?" Say, "What number minus two equals seven?" Test student suggestions in the box to see whether the sentence is true.

Group 1 ○

Reinforce Operations
1. Use counters and a number line to practice adding and subtracting numbers. Write the following math sentence, including a symbol: $9 + \stackrel{\wedge}{\star} = 15$.
2. Find and mark 9 and 15 on the number line. Ask, "Is this an addition or subtraction sentence? How do you know? Does that mean I move to the right or left on the number line?"
3. Count the spaces between the marked numbers. Substitute 6 for the symbol and model how to check whether the sentence is true.
4. Follow the same steps with a subtraction sentence: $\square - 3 = 5$. Mark the given numbers and prompt students to examine the operation sign. Ask, "What does the subtraction sign mean? Will the symbol number be larger or smaller than 3? Larger or smaller than 5?"
5. Demonstrate how to work backward by starting at 5 and moving three spaces to the right. Explain how to check whether 8 makes the sentence true.

Group 2 □

Unknown Quantities
1. Write $\triangle + 8 = 22$ on chart paper.
2. Place 22 counters on the table. Ask, "How can we use the numbers we know to solve for the number we don't know? The symbol is for addition; should we add 8 more counters to find the missing value? Why or why not?" Let students take away 8 counters to find the value of the triangle. Ask, "How can we check our answer?"
3. Write $17 - \square = 8$ and follow the same steps, giving students 17 counters. Explain that in subtraction problems, the first number is the largest of the three. So, the symbol must stand for a number smaller than 17. Use the counters to find the number that makes the sentence true. Model how to check the answer by using the inverse operation. Provide an additional subtraction example with a symbol for the minuend instead of the subtrahend. Ask students how this changes their strategy.
4. Have students write in their math journals about strategies for finding the values of symbols in math sentences.

Group 3 △

Solve Equations
1. Cut index cards into squares. Have students write the numbers 1–20 on the squares. Include some symbol cards (box, circle, triangle), two operation signs (+ and –), and an equal sign.
2. Demonstrate how to use the squares to build a math sentence that includes a symbol. Read the math sentence aloud, saying "a number" for the symbol. Point out the operation sign. Model how to determine and check the answer.
3. Invite a student pair to use the squares to make an equation. Have another pair explain how to find the number that makes the sentence true.
4. Ask, "Does it matter where I put the symbol? If a number works for one equation, will it work for every combination using the same cards?" Experiment by moving the symbol to different locations and testing the equations to see whether the same number makes the sentence true.
5. Have students write equations that include a symbol in their math journals and explain how to find the value of the symbol.

CD-104562 © Carson-Dellosa

Name_____

Read each math sentence. Look at the answer choices in the bank. Write the number that makes the sentence true in the circle.

Answer Bank				
3	6	7	10	15
5	8	9	14	18

1. $2 + \bigcirc = 9$

2. $5 + \bigcirc = 11$

3. $\bigcirc - 3 = 7$

4. $15 - \bigcirc = 12$

5. $\bigcirc - 5 = 4$

6. $8 + \bigcirc = 13$

7. $14 - \bigcirc = 6$

8. $\bigcirc + 9 = 24$

9. $16 + \bigcirc = 34$

10. $\bigcirc - 9 = 5$

Name_____

Read each math sentence. Write the value of the symbol that makes the sentence true. Write the math sentence you used to solve for the symbol.

1. $12 +$ △ $= 20$ △ $=$ _____ _____

2. ☆ $+ 23 = 27$ ☆ $=$ _____ _____

3. $14 - 9 =$ ☐   ☐ $=$ _____ _____

4. $32 +$ ◯ $= 41$ ◯ $=$ _____ _____

5. $11 -$ ◇ $= 5$ ◇ $=$ _____ _____

6. ☾ $+ 13 = 25$ ☾ $=$ _____ _____

7. $19 +$ ♡ $= 26$ ♡ $=$ _____ _____

8. ✿ $- 8 = 8$ ✿ $=$ _____ _____

9. $42 -$ ⬠ $= 20$ ⬠ $=$ _____ _____

10. ▭ $+ 17 = 30$ ▭ $=$ _____ _____

11. $52 +$ ❁ $= 86$ ❁ $=$ _____ _____

12. $24 -$ ☀ $= 9$ ☀ $=$ _____ _____

56

Name_____

Read each group of math sentences. Write one number that makes all three sentences true. Then, write an equation below each group using the same symbol and value.

1. $6 + \square = 20$

   $\square - 5 = 9$

   $8 + 6 = \square$

   $\square = $ _____

2. $\triangle - 3 = 3$

   $18 - \triangle = 12$

   $23 + \triangle = 29$

   $\triangle = $ _____

3. $38 + \bigcirc = 43$

   $\bigcirc + 9 = 14$

   $12 - \bigcirc = 7$

   $\bigcirc = $ _____

4. $27 - 18 = \stackrel{\star}{}$

   $19 + \stackrel{\star}{} = 28$

   $\stackrel{\star}{} + 6 = 15$

   $\stackrel{\star}{} = $ _____

5. $35 - \diamondsuit = 23$

   $\diamondsuit + 12 = 24$

   $40 - \diamondsuit = 28$

   $\diamondsuit = $ _____

6. $\heartsuit + 24 = 32$

   $13 + \heartsuit = 21$

   $42 - 34 = \heartsuit$

   $\heartsuit = $ _____

7. $\hexagon + 16 = 23$

   $\hexagon - 5 = 2$

   $35 + \hexagon = 42$

   $\hexagon = $ _____

8. $51 - \trapezoid = 47$

   $\trapezoid + 31 = 35$

   $30 - 26 = \trapezoid$

   $\trapezoid = $ _____

9. $\pentagon \times 6 = 18$

   $12 \div \pentagon = 4$

   $9 \times \pentagon = 27$

   $\pentagon = $ _____

10. $24 \div \bigcirc = 4$

    $\bigcirc \times 10 = 60$

    $36 \div \bigcirc = 0$

    $\bigcirc = $ _____

Measurement

Materials:
- Balance scale
- Counters
- Miscellaneous objects (to weigh)
- Chart paper
- Activity sheets (pages 59–61)
- Math journals

Objective
Use nonstandard units to measure the weight of an object.

Mini-Lesson

1. Describe the term *measurement* as a way of comparing things (longer or shorter, lighter or heavier). Discuss the variety of things students measure in their daily lives: lengths, temperatures, quantities, weights.
2. Demonstrate how to use a balance scale. Explain that when two objects weigh the same, the scale balances. Place an object on one side of the scale and an identical object on the other side. Place a different object on one side of the scale and point out how the scale tips. When one object is heavier than the other, the scale is lower on the heavier side.
3. Model how to use a nonstandard unit (counters) to measure the weight of an object. Place the object on one side of the scale. Add counters to the other side. Continue to add counters until the scale balances.
4. Measure several objects with counters. Compare and order the weights of the objects.

Group 1 ○

Practice Measuring
1. Use a nonstandard unit, such as counters, to measure three classroom objects (pencil, eraser, student scissors).
2. Explain that a *nonstandard unit* is a measurement tool that is not universally agreed upon, unlike an inch or centimeter.
3. Model how to use the balance scale to find the weight of the objects using counters. Place an object on one side. Add counters to the other side until the scale balances. Record the number of counters each object weighs.
4. Order the weights. Compare the objects in terms of their weights in counters. Ask, "Which object is the lightest? Which object is the heaviest? How can you tell?"
5. Have students write in their math journals about using a balance scale.

Group 2 □

Comparing Units
1. Select several small objects from the classroom. Use the balance scale to find the weight of classroom objects using counters as the nonstandard measuring unit. Then, measure the weights of the same objects using a different nonstandard unit such as identical paper clips, erasers, or beans.
2. Record the weights of the measured objects on chart paper. Ask, "Why does the same object have different weights when I use different nonstandard units? Does it mean the object is suddenly heavier or lighter?"
3. Discuss how measurement can appear different depending on the kind of unit used. An object might weigh a larger number of units if the measuring unit is light. There may be a smaller number of units when the measurement unit is heavier. Ask, "Why do you think such units are nonstandard and not used as typical measurements?"
4. Have students write in their math journals about the use of nonstandard units.

Group 3 △

Appropriate Measurements
1. Have students choose several items from the classroom to weigh on the balance scale. Choose a variety of light and heavy objects. Select multiple nonstandard units.
2. Place an object on the scale. Ask, "Which of our nonstandard units should be used to measure this object? Does it make sense to weigh a textbook with paper clips? What would be a better unit of measurement?"
3. Challenge students to weigh all of the objects, choosing the units of measurement that will require the least number of units to weigh each object.
4. Discuss how measurement can appear different depending on the kind of unit used. Emphasize how using tools that do not use standard measurements can affect results. Ask, "How can we choose which unit of measurement to use? Why is it useful to choose measurement units that will provide us with smaller numbers?"
5. Have students write in their math journals about choosing appropriate nonstandard units.

Name_____

Look at each scale. Circle the group of marbles that makes the scale true.

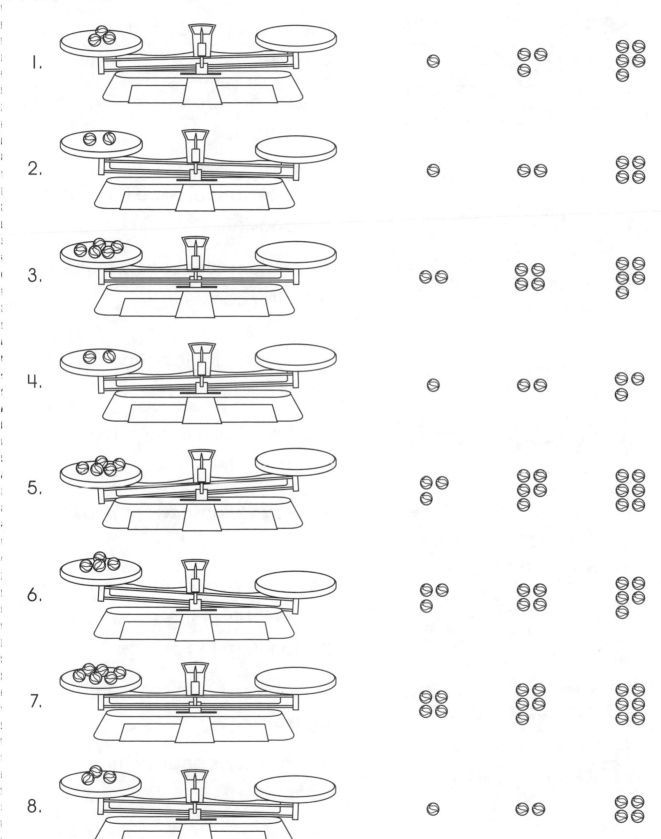

Name_____

Look at the pictures. Circle each true sentence.

1.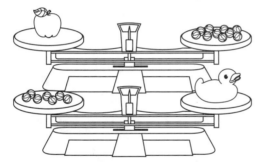

The eraser is heavier than the roll of tape.

The roll of tape weighs more than the eraser.

2.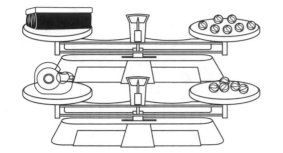

The watermelon slice is lighter than the cookie.

The watermelon slice weighs more than the cookie.

3.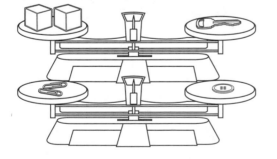

The toy weighs less than the apple.

The toy is heavier than the apple.

4.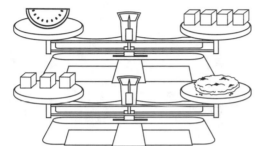

The key weighs the same as the button.

You cannot accurately compare the weights of the key and the button from the picture.

5.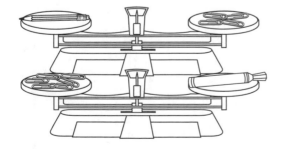

The pencil is heavier than the marker.

The marker is heavier than the pencil.

Name_____

Look at each picture. Circle the best unit to weigh each object.

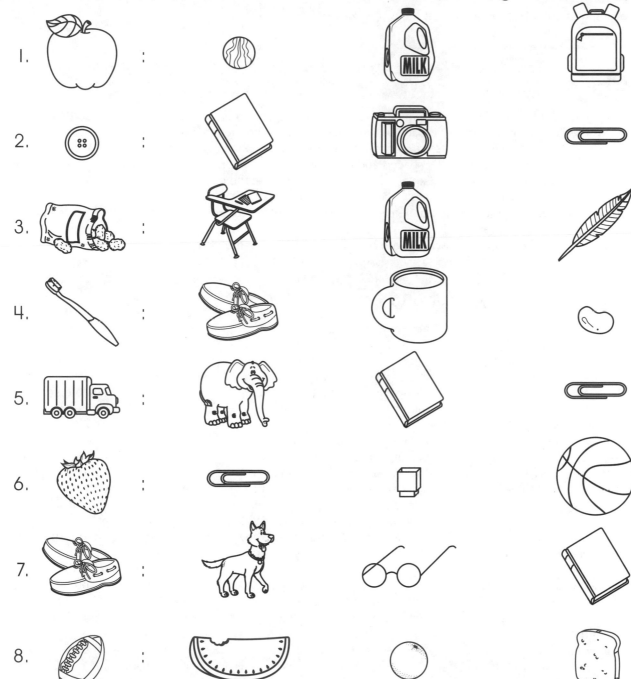

Answer the question.

9. Does it make sense to use the measurement units shown above in real life? Explain.

_____

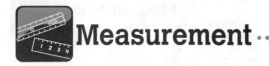

Measurement

Materials:
- Centimeter and inch rulers
- Activity sheets (pages 63–65)
- Math journals

Objective
Measure the length of an object to the nearest inch and centimeter.

Mini-Lesson

1. Examine a standard ruler together. Explain that rulers are made with the exact same measurements so that comparisons are consistent. If using a human foot, for example, measured lengths would vary and depend on the size of the foot. Because measurements are standard for everyone, comparisons are more accurate.
2. Point out how the inch marks are exactly spaced and the unit marks between the numbers show parts of an inch. Compare this with the centimeter ruler. Explain that some countries use the customary units (inches), while other countries use the metric system (centimeters).
3. Model how to measure an object. Line up the first line (0) on the ruler with the end of an object. Always start with the end that has the number 1, like a number line.
4. Practice measuring objects in the classroom with both the inch and centimeter rulers.

Group 1 ○
Reinforce Technique
1. Ask, "What are the standard measurements for the customary system? The metric system?"
2. Look at the unit marks on a ruler. Point out that the inch marks are spaced exactly the same distance apart. Compare the customary and metric system rulers. Ask, "How many units does a customary ruler show? How many units does a metric ruler show?"
3. Model how to line up the first line on the ruler with the end of a classroom object. Remind students to always start with the end printed with 1 but not line up the object starting at 1. Lay the ruler on a flat surface against the top of the object and find its measurement. Round to the nearest whole inch.
4. Follow the same steps to measure objects in centimeters to the nearest whole centimeter. Let students practice measuring other objects. Highlight the ease and accuracy in comparison with nonstandard units.
5. Have students list the steps to measure an object with a ruler in their math journals.

Group 2 □
Practice Measuring
1. Compare a customary and metric ruler. Ask, "How many inches are on a customary ruler? How many centimeters are on a metric ruler? Are the centimeter units larger or smaller than the inch units? About how many centimeters are in one inch?"
2. Model how to measure in inches a classroom object, like a pencil. Remind students how to line up a ruler. Explain to students that if a measurement is not exact, they should say the object is "about" that many inches.
3. Introduce the measurement abbreviations for inches (in.) and centimeters (cm). Ask, "Does it make a difference if I forget to write the unit label after the measurement? How does the label affect the measurement?"
4. Draw a straight line on chart paper. Ask volunteers to measure the length with both rulers. Encourage students to explain their thought processes and describe their measurements.
5. Have students write in their math journals about the importance of accuracy and labels when measuring length.

Group 3 △
Practical Measuring
1. Compare a customary and metric ruler. Ask, "How many inches are on a customary ruler? How many centimeters are on a metric ruler? Are the centimeter units larger or smaller than the inch units? About how many centimeters are in one inch?"
2. Draw lines of various lengths, including those that are not exact lengths and those that are longer than 12 inches. Invite volunteers to measure the lengths with both rulers. Challenge students to deal with in-between measurements and lengths greater than 12 inches. Ask, "Should I round up or down? Can I use a half inch? How can I use the same ruler to measure a line that is longer than the ruler?"
3. Model how to draw a line of a given length (5 cm). Label the line with the correct units.
4. Let students practice drawing lines of differing lengths in their math journals. Let students switch with partners to measure and label.

Name_____

Measure each object to the nearest whole unit. Write the length in inches and centimeters.

1.
_____ in.

_____ cm

2.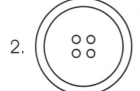
_____ in.

_____ cm

3.
_____ in.

_____ cm

4.
_____ in.

_____ cm

5.
_____ in.

_____ cm

6.
_____ in.

_____ cm

7.
_____ in.

_____ cm

8.
_____ in.

_____ cm

Name_____

Choose the more reasonable length for each object. Measure each object to the nearest inch or centimeter.

1.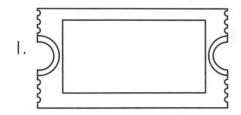

2 inches or 2 centimeters?

actual measurement: _____

2.

4 inches or 4 centimeters?

actual measurement: _____

3.

4 inches or 4 centimeters?

actual measurement: _____

4.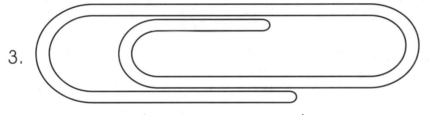

3 inches or 3 centimeters?

actual measurement: _____

5.

2 inches or 2 centimeters?

actual measurement: _____

6.

3 inches or 3 centimeters?

actual measurement: _____

CD-104562 © Carson-Dellosa

Name_____

Draw a line for each length. Then, answer the questions.

1. 4 in.

2. 8 cm

3. 2 in.

4. 3 in.

5. 5 cm

6. 4 cm

7. $5\frac{1}{2}$ in.

8. 6 cm

9. How many times would you have to move your ruler to measure an object that was 30 inches long?

_____

_____

10. How many times would you have to move your ruler to measure an object that was 30 centimeters long?

_____

_____

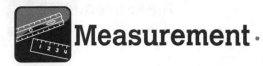 **Measurement** · · · · · · · · · · · · · ·

Materials:
- Chart paper
- Analog clock manipulative
- Digital clock
- Activity sheets (pages 67–69)
- Math journals

Objective
Tell time to the nearest quarter hour and know time relationships.

Mini-Lesson

1. Show a digital clock and explain that the hour is first and the minutes are second. Point out the colon that separates the hours and the minutes. The minutes on a digital clock can be 00–59; the hours on a digital clock can be 1–12. After 12, the hour starts over at 1.
2. Show an analog clock. Model the clockwise direction of time. Point out how the large numbers indicate hours, while the smaller lines between numbers show minutes. The numbers are written at each five-minute mark.
3. Explain that the short hand points to the hour and the long hand points to the minute. Demonstrate how the hour hand moves slowly toward the next hour as the minutes get closer to 60.
4. Show various times to the quarter hour on both analog and digital clocks and let students read the time. Then, have students show matching digital and analog clocks.

Group 1 ○

Basic Concepts

1. Write the following times on chart paper: 1:30, 6:15, 45:11, 7:00. Read each time aloud. Ask, "Which time is not written correctly?" Review the structure of hours : minutes. Practice writing and reading digital times.
2. Examine an analog clock together. Begin at 12 and practice moving the minute hand while counting by 5s. Point out the top of the hour, quarter after, half past, and quarter till, and the corresponding number and minutes for each location.
3. Point out how the hour hand moves more slowly than the minute hand. When the hour hand is between hours, use the smaller of those numbers to name the hour.
4. Say a time aloud and have students draw or show the time on an analog clock and write the matching digital time.
5. Have students define the terms *hands, minutes, hours, clock,* and *time* in their math journals.

Group 2 □

Practice Reading Clocks

1. Write a digital time on chart paper. Ask a student to read the time aloud. Ask, "How do you know which number is the hour and which is the minutes?"
2. Discuss the concept of A.M. and P.M. Brainstorm common activities that take place in mornings, afternoons, evenings, and nights. Write example digital times for each activity.
3. Draw a simple analog clock on chart paper. Draw lines dividing the circle into equal fourths. Ask, "Why do we call 15 minutes past the hour quarter after? Where is the minute hand when the time is quarter past the hour? Where is the minute hand when the time is half past the hour? Three-quarters past the hour or quarter till the next hour?"
4. Show times to the quarter hour on both an analog clock and a digital clock. Have students practice naming the times with both minutes and using the more familiar "half past," "quarter past," and "quarter till."
5. Have students describe in their math journals how to tell time to the nearest 15 minutes.

Group 3 △

Time Relationships

1. Ask, "How many minutes are in one hour?" Practice counting by 5s to 60. Ask, "How do multiples of 5 connect with telling time? How can you use the clock numbers and multiples of 5 to determine the minutes instead of counting by 5s?"
2. Model various times and have students count by 5s to determine how many minutes after the hour it is. Ask, "How else can you tell time past the half hour mark?" Model how to count by 5s backward from 12 to tell the number of minutes before the next hour.
3. Discuss how to count elapsed time. Give an example of an activity starting and ending at specific times. Use multiples of five to count the minutes between the start and end times. Challenge students to determine elapsed time across the top of the hour and across A.M./P.M. times.
4. Have students write in their math journals about time relationships and elapsed time.

Name_____

Look at the time on each digital clock. Write the letter of the matching analog clock.

1. _____    A.

2. _____    B.

3. _____    C.

4. _____    D.

5. _____    E.

6. _____    F.

Name_____

Look at each clock. Write the time.

1.

_____

2.

_____

3.

_____

4.

_____

5.

_____

6.

_____

7.

_____

8.

_____

9.

_____

Write each time in words.

10.  7:45

_____

11.  10:30

_____

12.  12:15

_____

Name_____

Write the time under each clock. Write the number of minutes after the hour as a multiplication sentence.

1.  _____

_____

2.  _____

_____

3.  _____

_____

Determine the elapsed time for each problem below.

4. Jon left for school at 7:25. He arrived at school at 7:40. How long did it take Jon to walk to school?

5. Soccer practice starts at 3:30. It finishes at 4:15. How long is soccer practice?

6. Paige puts a casserole in the oven at 5:20. It is done baking at 5:50. How long was the casserole in the oven?

 # Geometry

Materials:
- Tangrams
- Crayons
- Activity sheets (pages 70–73)
- Math journals

Objective
Identify and name regular two-dimensional objects.

Mini-Lesson

1. Draw and label the following shapes on the board: square, rectangle, triangle, hexagon, octagon, rhombus, trapezoid, and parallelogram. Point out the attributes of each shape. Introduce vocabulary terms such as side, straight, curve, and vertex.
2. Brainstorm examples of each shape in students' environments. Ask them to think about the classroom, school, playground, and home.
3. Compare and contrast the polygons. Ask, "Which shape has three straight sides? How many sides does a hexagon have? How many vertices does a square have?"
4. Use tangrams to reinforce shape names and attributes. Move the tangrams in different positions so that students recognize shapes in different forms.

Group 1 ○

Recognize Basic Shapes
1. Use tangrams to identify and reinforce recognition of the shapes from the mini-lesson.
2. Choose a triangle. Ask, "Are the sides of this shape straight or curved? How many sides are there? What is the name of this shape?" Have students find matching triangle tangrams.
3. Follow the same process for each shape. Reinforce math vocabulary with descriptions of each shape. Ask, "Which shape has a curved side? Which shape has six sides? What is the shape name of a stop sign?"
4. Model how to trace a tangram shape on a piece of paper. Demonstrate how to reposition it and trace it again so that students learn to recognize the same shapes in different positions. Label each group of shapes with their correct names. Ask, "Does the size of a figure change its basic shape? Does the way the figure is turned or positioned change its basic shape?"
5. Have students list each shape with one defining attribute in their math journals.

Group 2 ▢

Classify 2-D Shapes
1. Use tangrams to classify the shapes from the mini-lesson.
2. Compare and contrast the shapes. Reinforce math vocabulary with descriptions of each shape. Ask, "How are a triangle and a square alike? How are they different? Which two-dimensional shape is unlike the rest of the list? How is it different?"
3. Help students create lists of rules for each shape. For example, a square must have 4 sides, each side must be the same length, and each corner must be a right angle. Ask, "Do any shapes share some of the same rules?"
4. Let students experiment with flipping, sliding, and turning the shapes. Let students experiment with tangrams. Introduce the term *congruent*. Ask, "Are the shapes still congruent after flipping, sliding or turning them?" Have students draw different sizes of shapes. Ask, "Are the differently sized shapes congruent?"
5. Have students draw and label three shapes used during the lesson in their math journals.

Group 3 △

Distinguish 2-D Geometry
1. Compare and contrast the quadrilaterals. Discuss the number and length of sides and whether opposite sides are parallel. Ask, "How are a rectangle and a parallelogram alike? How are they different? How are trapezoids similar to parallelograms? How are they different?"
2. Introduce the term *symmetrical*. Ask, "Which shape is the most symmetrical? The least?"
3. Use tangrams to model how some basic two-dimensional figures can be made up of two other basic shapes reflected over a line of symmetry. For example, a right triangle reflected to make a square, or a square reflected to make a rectangle.
4. Let students trace reflections of tangrams with one color and trace the outline of the larger symmetrical figure with a different color. Identify the figure and the shapes within the figure.
5. Have students write in their math journals about symmetrical figures and draw examples of shapes made from the reflection of smaller shapes.

Name_____

Follow the directions to color the shapes.

1. Color the triangles green.

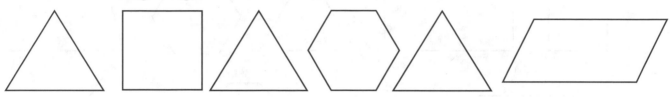

2. Color the hexagons blue.

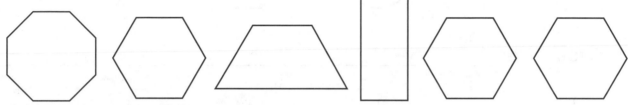

3. Color the trapezoids purple.

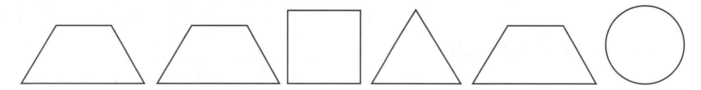

4. Color the octagons red.

5. Color the rectangles yellow.

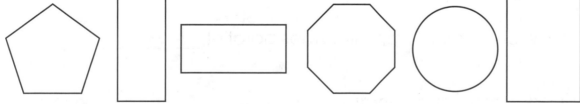

6. Color the circles orange.

Name_____

Write the letter or letters of each shape described.

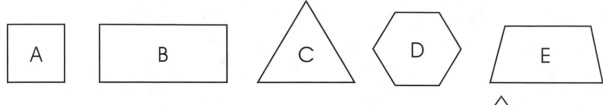

1. has four sides _____

2. has six vertices_____

3. has no straight sides _____

4. has more than five sides_____

5. has at least three vertices _____

6. shape of a stop sign _____

7. must have one pair of opposite sides parallel _____

8. all four sides are equal length _____

9. has less than four vertices _____

10. is a two-dimensional shape _____

Name_____

Draw a line of symmetry to show the reflected shape inside each main figure. Write the names of the main figure and the reflected shape.

1.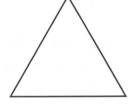

main figure: _____

reflected shape: _____

2.

main figure: _____

reflected shape: _____

3.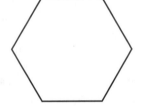

main figure: _____

reflected shape: _____

4.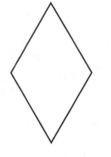

main figure: _____

reflected shape: _____

5.

main figure: _____

reflected shape: _____

6.

main figure: _____

reflected shape: _____

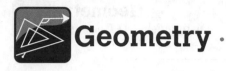

Geometry

Materials:
- Set of solid figures
- Crayons
- Activity sheets (pages 75–77)
- Math journals

Objective
Describe and classify solid figures.

Mini-Lesson

1. Draw a square, rectangle, triangle, and circle. Identify these shapes as *plane figures*. (They have a flat surface.)
2. Show models of a sphere, cone, cylinder, rectangular prism, square pyramid, and cube. Identify these as three-dimensional, or *solid*, figures. Challenge students to try to find examples of each solid in their school environment.
3. Compare and contrast the solids. Describe the attributes of each shape using the terms *edge*, *face*, and *vertex*.
4. Show each figure and identify each of its *faces*. Emphasize that solid figures can have differently shaped faces on the same solid. Hold the solid from each angle to focus on one side at a time.
5. Point out the number of *vertices*, touching each one as you count. Run your finger along each *edge* to identify where two faces of the solid meet. Determine which solids have curved sides by testing to see which ones roll.

Group 1 ○

Recognize Faces on Solids

1. Focus on the faces of a solid. Model how to place a solid face down on a piece of paper and trace it. Do this for each face. Examine the shapes.
2. Ask, "How many faces does this solid have? Are all of the faces the same shape? What is the name of each shape?" Follow the same process and make a list of the face shapes found on each solid.
3. Reinforce that a face is a flat surface. Some solids have a curved surface (cylinder, cone, sphere). Test whether each solid can roll smoothly to identify curved surfaces.
4. Place three solids in a group. Ask comparing and contrasting questions. "Which shape has two circular faces? Which shape has six square faces? Which shape has no faces?"
5. Have students write in their math journals about the faces of solids.

Group 2 □

Classify Solids

1. Focus on the terms used to describe and classify solids (*face, edge, vertex*). Examine and identify each face of the solids together. Count the number of edges and vertices.
2. Compare and contrast the solids. Reinforce math vocabulary with descriptions of each shape. Ask, "How are a cone and a cylinder alike? Different? Which solids can roll and why? How are a square pyramid and triangular prism alike? Different?"
3. Practice sorting the solids by a given criteria. Ask, "Which solids have a triangular face? Which solids have a square face? Which solids have a circular face? Which solids have five or more vertices? Which solid is unlike the rest? How is it different? Which solids have more than 8 edges?"
4. Have students write a reflection in their math journals. Encourage them to identify a solid by the number of faces, edges, and vertices.

Group 3 △

Differentiate Solids

1. Have students hold each solid. Direct them to touch and identify each face shape. Encourage them to run their fingers along each edge and touch each vertex as they count the attributes of each solid.
2. Place the solids in an opaque bag. Let students take turns closing their eyes, choosing a block, and trying to identify it just by touch.
3. After each student has had a turn, instruct students to write riddles for each solid using the appropriate vocabulary. For example, "I am similar to a cube, but my faces may not all have equal length sides."
4. Let students practice solving each other's riddles.
5. Challenge students to select one solid and write a commercial with selling points for the figure in their math journals.

Name_____

Follow the directions to color each solid. Write the name on the line.

Solid Names		
sphere	triangular pyramid	rectangular prism
cone	cylinder	

1. Color the solid that has two circle faces.

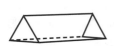   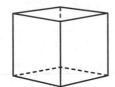   

Solid:_____

2. Color the solid that has no faces.

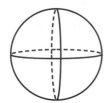      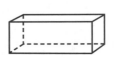

Solid:_____

3. Color the solid that has at least four rectangle faces.

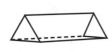   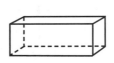

Solid:_____

4. Color the solid that has four triangle faces.

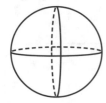   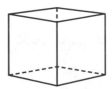

Solid:_____

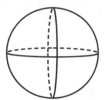  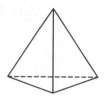 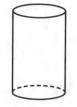 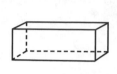 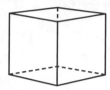

| sphere | cone | triangular pyramid | cylinder | rectangular prism | cube |

Look at each solid above. Then, complete the chart.

Name of Solid	Number of Faces	Shape of Faces	Number of Vertices	Number of Edges
1.	1	circle	1	1, curved
2.		square	8	12
3. rectangular prism		rectangle, square	8	
4.			4	
5. cylinder		circle	0	2, curved
6.	0	no faces		0

Name_____

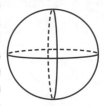

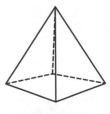

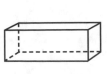
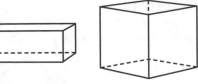

sphere   cone   square pyramid   cylinder   rectangular prism   cube

Write the name of the solid that matches each description.

1. I have six square faces.

_____

2. I have one circular face and one curved surface.

_____

3. I have five faces and five vertices.

_____

4. I have no faces, edges, or vertices.

_____

5. I have at least four rectangular faces and 12 vertices.

_____

6. I have two faces and one curved surface.

_____

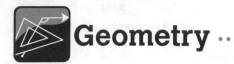 # Geometry

Objective

Compose and decompose two-dimensional shapes.

Materials:
- Chart paper
- Tangrams (or pattern blocks)
- Scissors
- Construction paper
- Activity sheets (pages 79–81)
- Math journals

Mini-Lesson

1. Draw the following shapes on chart paper: square, rectangle, triangle, parallelogram, trapezoid, circle, rhombus, hexagon, and octagon. Identify and label each shape.
2. Model how to use tangrams to build two-dimensional shapes. Place two shapes together, such as a square and a triangle, to make a house shape. Explain how together they build a new shape.
3. Look around for plane figures composed of more than one shape. Draw and identify the shapes within the figures.
4. Then, draw a right trapezoid on the board. Model how to cut this shape into smaller geometric shapes, such as a square and a triangle or a parallelogram and a triangle. Try other shapes and see how many different ways students can divide the figures.

Group 1 ○

Shape Recognition

1. Review the two-dimensional shapes from the mini-lesson. Use math terminology to describe and compare the shapes.
2. Explain that the same shape can appear in different forms. Draw three different trapezoids on chart paper. Ask, "Are all of these trapezoids?" Draw lines creating shapes inside to point out that all three are trapezoids, but one has a square in the middle with identical triangles on each side, one is a rectangle with different triangles on each side, and one is a square with a triangle on the side.
3. Draw a hexagon. Divide it in half and discuss the shapes created within the hexagon. Divide the hexagon in another way to create different shapes. Ask, "Can I break apart this hexagon in other ways to make other new shapes?"
4. Have students draw shapes in their math journals and explain how to divide them into two other shapes.

Group 2 □

Compose Shapes

1. Find a template of a tangram pattern. Copy the template onto several pieces of construction paper. Distribute to students.
2. Identify the whole composed shape together, then have students cut along the lines to decompose the tangram pattern into its separate pieces. Challenge them to compose the pieces again. Let students play with tangram patterns for various pictures such as a clown, a dog, or a boat.
3. Model how to place two pieces together to create a typical shape. Ask, "What shape can two trapezoids create? (hexagon) Can you make the same shape with other tangram pieces? (rotated triangles)"
4. Challenge student pairs to use multiple tangram pieces to build larger plane shapes. For each composition, ask, "What is the name of the shape you created? What shapes did you use to build that figure? Did you have to turn, flip, or slide the shapes?"
5. Have students write in their math journals about composing two-dimensional shapes.

Group 3 △

Decompose Shapes

1. Ask volunteers to draw as many four-sided shapes as they can on chart paper. Sort and classify the shapes. Name the recognized quadrilaterals from the mini-lesson. Follow the same process with triangles.
2. Emphasize that hexagons and octagons can look very different from the typical example. Use two parallelogram tangram pieces to create the head of an arrow. Define a hexagon as a six-sided polygon. Classify the arrow as a hexagon, and challenge students to create other hexagonal figures.
3. Let students create their own polygons and divide them into smaller geometric shapes. Have them cut their shapes into the smaller shapes to make puzzles. Let students switch puzzles with partners to see if they can make the same original shapes or see what new shapes they can make.
4. Have students write in their math journals about composing and decomposing shapes. Ask them to include different examples of drawings of figures composed of different shapes.

Name_____

Draw lines inside each figure to create the shapes described.

1. 3 triangles

2. 2 triangles

 1 rectangle

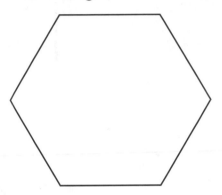

3. 1 triangle

 1 parallelogram

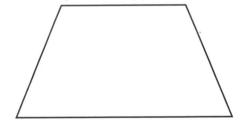

4. 1 trapezoid

 2 triangles

 1 rectangle

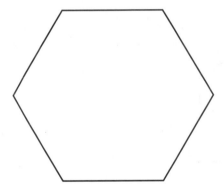

5. 1 triangle

 1 trapezoid

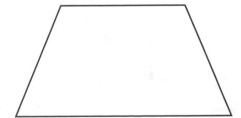

6. 1 rectangle

 2 trapezoids

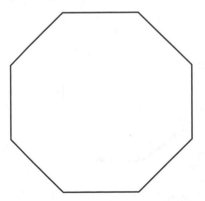

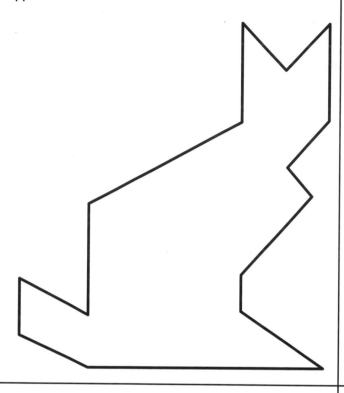

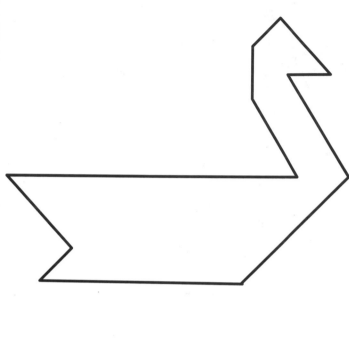

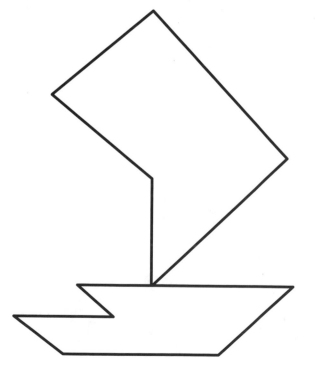

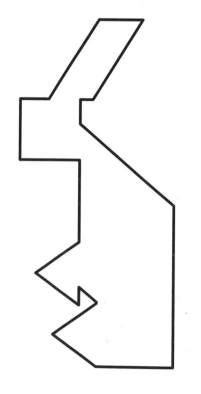

Name

Draw lines to fill each outline with tangram shapes.

1.

2.

3.

4.

Name_____

Use the listed tangrams to follow the directions. Draw or trace each new shape.

1. Use I square and I triangle to build a pentagon.

2. Use 2 triangles to build a parallelogram.

3. Use I parallelogram and I triangle to build a trapezoid.

4. Use 2 squares to build a rectangle.

5. Use I square and I triangle to build a trapezoid.

6. Use 2 triangles to build a square or rectangle.

Data Analysis and Probability

Objective
Collect, record, and interpret data using tables and tallies.

Materials:
- Multicolored counters
- Jar of pennies, nickels, dimes, and quarters
- Activity sheets (pages 83–85)
- Math journals

Mini-Lesson

1. Discuss the math terms *data, table, tally*, and *survey*. Explain that a *survey* is a way to gather information on a topic. The answers from the survey are the data, or information. This can be represented by tallies in a table.
2. Draw a table on the board. Ask, "What kinds of pets do you have at home?" Decide together what the categories will be (for example, dog, cat, other, no pets). Ask, "Why do we need to provide categories to choose from? What happens to our results if we don't give a few choices?"
3. Label the table columns with headers (*Pet Type, Tally Marks, Total Number*). Ask students to draw tally marks in the columns to show their answers. Explain that this is an easy way to quickly count the total number later.
4. Demonstrate how to write the total number for each pet in the table. Discuss the results of the survey together.

Group 1 ○

Organize Data
1. Gather a large pile of multicolored counters. Draw a table with column headers *Color, Tally Marks*, and *Total Number*. Under *Color*, write the names of the counter colors.
2. Explain that tables organize information so that it is easy to understand quickly. This table will show the number of each color of counters. Have students sort the counters by color. Model how to draw a tally mark in the middle column for each counter.
3. Show how the data is organized by rows. Explain that each tally mark stands for 1 counter. Point out how the tallies are grouped by 5s for easier counting. Write the total number of tallies for each color on the same row in the last column.
4. Ask, "Which color had the most counters? Which color had the fewest counters? What is the purpose of using tallies? Why did we also write the total number?"
5. Have students copy the table in their math journals.

Group 2 □

Read Tables
1. Draw a table with column headers *Birthday Month* and *Number of Students*. Under *Birthday Month*, write answer choices *March, April, May*, and *June*. Write 7 tallies for March, 2 for April, 11 for May, and 5 for June.
2. Ask, "How can I tell what kind of data the table holds and what it means?" Point out the column headers and row categories. Ask, "What would be a good title for this table?"
3. Have volunteers count the tally marks and write the total number of students for each month in the table. Emphasize that all of the data in each row goes together. Ask, "How could I find the total number of birthdays in March and May? What can I do to find how many more students had a birthday in June than in April?"
4. Have students copy the table in their math journals. Ask each student to write two questions about the data and write the corresponding answers.

Group 3 △

Create Tables
1. Present a jar of mixed coins. Tell students to create a table to display the different types of coins in the jar. Ask, "What column headers will you need? What categories will you have? What title will you use?"
2. Help students draw the table. Include a column for tallies. Have students sort the coins by denomination. Mark a tally for each coin sorted. Ask, "How does writing the tallies in groups of 5's help you organize the information?" Direct students to write the total number of each coin in the table.
3. Examine the data together. Ask, "How many pennies and dimes are there in all? How many more quarters than nickels are there? Using the table, how can I find the total number of coins in the container?" Discuss how word clues such as "in all" or "how many more" signal which operation to use.
4. Have students copy the table in their math journals. Ask them to write three questions about the data and write the answers to their questions.

Name_____

Colin took a survey of his classmates' favorite fruits and sports.
Record the data in each table.

Fruit	Tally Marks	Total Number
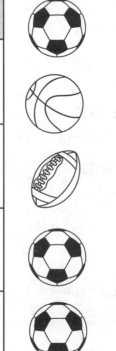		

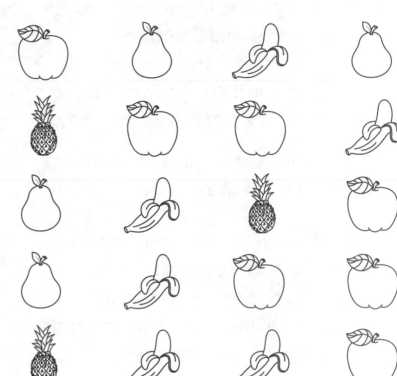

Sport	Tally Marks	Total Number

Name_____

Read each paragraph. Record the data in the tables.

1. Grace sells T-shirts. On Monday, she sold 3 large and 4 medium shirts. On Tuesday, she sold 5 small and 2 large shirts. On Thursday, she sold 1 medium and 4 large shirts. She sold 3 small and 2 large shirts on Friday.

   How many T-shirts did Grace sell this week in each size?

T-shirt Size	Tally Marks	Total Number

2. Jacob plays on a traveling hockey team. In August, his team won 6 games and lost 3 games. In September, they tied 2 games and won 5 games. In October, the team won 4 games and lost 2 games. They lost 3 games and won 3 games in December.

   By winter break, what was the team's record?

Game Outcome	Tally Marks	Total Number

3. In classroom A, 8 students ride the bus to school and 4 students arrive by car. In classroom B, 3 students walk and 9 others ride the bus. In classroom C, 2 students arrive by car, 7 ride the bus, and 3 walk.

   How many second-grade students take each form of transportation?

Travel Method	Tally Marks	Total Number

84

Name_____

Write three questions with answer choices to ask your classmates. Perform the surveys or create your own data. Record the data in the tables.

Question: _____

_____

Answer Choices	Tally Marks	Total

Question: _____

_____

Answer Choices	Tally Marks	Total

Question: _____

_____

Answer Choices	Tally Marks	Total

Data Analysis and Probability

Materials:
- Multicolored cubes
- Crayons
- Construction paper
- Activity sheets (pages 87–89)
- Math journals

Objective
Collect, record, and interpret data using bar graphs.

Mini-Lesson

1. Explain the term *graph*. Tell students a graph shows information. Each bar in a bar graph stands for a number.
2. Ask students to take a sheet of construction paper that represents their favorite color. Build a whole-class bar graph on a classroom wall. Help students organize their papers in groups by color.
3. Label numbers along the vertical axis and color names along the horizontal axis. Model how to read the graph when all students have posted their papers on the wall. Demonstrate how to follow the top of each color bar to the number on the left.
4. Model how to compare the heights of the bars. Ask, "Which color is liked the most? How many students like yellow? Do more students like blue or green? How many more?" Use vocabulary like *most, more than,* and *total*.

Group 1 ○

Create Bar Graphs
1. Collect 20 multicolored cubes. Have students sort and stack the cubes by color. Arrange each stack to look like a bar on a bar graph.
2. Draw a bar graph on a piece of paper. Write the name of each color of cube along the bottom. Have students arrange their stacks correctly on the graph.
3. Write numbers along the left side of the graph to match the size of the cubes. Discuss how the numbers start at 0 and go up by 1 like a number line.
4. Model how to compare the stacks. Ask, "Which color has the biggest bar? Which color has the smallest bar? What does that mean?" Explain that the taller the bar, the bigger the number.
5. Practice connecting the numbers and color names. Ask, "Which color has 4 cubes? How many cubes are red? How many blue and red cubes are there?"

Group 2 □

Read Bar Graphs
1. Draw the two axes of a bar graph on the board. Title the graph *After-School Activities*. Label the categories on the x-axis *Art, Computer, Music,* and *Sports*. Write a scale in increments of 2 on the y-axis.
2. Draw bars to represent the number of students who reported their favorite after-school activity: art (3), computer (6), music (4), sports (9). Model how to follow the top of a bar to the number of students.
3. Interpret the data together. Ask, "What does it mean when the top of a bar falls between two lines on the scale? How many students are involved in each activity? What do I do to find how many more students play sports than create art? How do I find the number of students who use the computer or take a music class after school? How would I find the total number of students who reported their favorite activity?"
4. Have students copy the graph in their math journals and write three facts that it shows.

Group 3 △

Analyze Bar Graphs
1. Draw a double bar graph titled *Summer Soccer Program* on chart paper. Draw a scale with intervals of 2 and write three labels on the x-axis for years (2010, 2011, 2012). Draw two bars for each year: 2010 boys (12) and girls (5), 2011 boys (10) and girls (8), and 2012 boys (9) and girls (12). Shade the bars for girls in each year.
2. Draw a key and explain how to tell the two groups of data apart on the bar graph. Ask, "Why is one bar shaded for each year? How many years are shown on the graph? What information does the graph show?"
3. Discuss how to interpret the information. Ask, "In 2011, how can you find the total number of girls and boys who participated in the summer soccer program? How can you find how many more boys played soccer in 2010 than in 2012? In which year did more girls than boys participate in the soccer program?"
4. Have students copy the double bar graph in their math journals. Challenge them to write and answer questions about the data.

Name_____

Look at the table. Create a bar graph from the data. Then, answer the questions.

Dessert	Total Orders
Brownie	10
Ice Cream	6
Pie	7

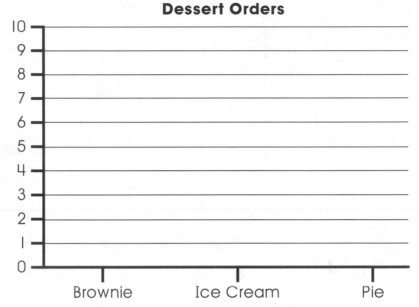

Dessert Orders

A waitress kept a tally of the kinds of desserts ordered by her customers.

1. How many customers ordered a piece of pie? _____

2. Which dessert was ordered the most? _____

3. Which dessert was ordered the least? _____

4. How many more customers ordered a brownie than ice cream?_____

5. How many total customers ordered ice cream or pie? _____

6. How many customers in all ordered a dessert? _____

Name_____

Look at the graph. Answer the questions.

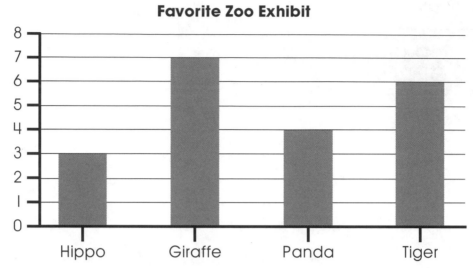

After a field trip, students voted for their favorite zoo exhibit.

1. Which exhibit got the most votes? _____

2. How many students voted for the exhibit with the most votes? _____

3. What does it mean when the bar is between two numbers on the scale?

   _____

   _____

4. How can you tell which exhibit was more popular—the panda or the tiger?

   _____

   _____

5. How many more students liked the giraffe exhibit than the hippo exhibit?

   _____

6. How many students liked the giraffe and tiger exhibits in all? _____

88

Name_____

Look at the graph. Answer the questions.

Favorite Ice Cream Flavors

An ice cream shop kept track of the ice cream orders one weekend.

1. Which flavor was most popular on Saturday?_____

2. How many customers ordered that flavor on Saturday? _____

3. How many total customers ordered strawberry ice cream
   this weekend? _____

4. On Sunday, how many more customers ordered vanilla than
   butter pecan? _____

5. How many customers ordered the two most popular flavors on
   Saturday? _____

6. How can you tell which flavor was the least favorite this weekend?

   _____

   _____

7. How many total customers were served on Saturday? _____

8. How many more total customers were served on Sunday than
   Saturday? _____

Data Analysis and Probability

Materials:
- Chart paper
- Construction paper
- Scissors
- Counters
- Activity sheets (pages 91–93)
- Math journals

Objective

Interpret data representation and answer related questions.

Mini-Lesson

1. Define *pictograph*. Explain that these kinds of graphs display information, similar to bar graphs. Instead of bars, a picture is used to stand for a number. Pictographs have a key that tells the number each picture represents.
2. Draw a pictograph on the board. Label the graph *Trading Cards*. Create four rows and write the names *Chase, Delinda, Felipe*, and *Isabelle* along the left side of the graph. Include a key that shows 1 counter means 1 trading card. Place 6 counters in the row for Chase, 4 for Delinda, 5 for Felipe, and 7 for Isabelle.
3. Ask, "How many trading cards does Chase have? Does Delinda have more or less trading cards than Felipe? Can you tell without counting? Which student has 4 trading cards? Which student has the most trading cards? How many total trading cards does this group have?" Emphasize vocabulary like *most, more than,* and *total*.

Group 1 ○

Read Pictographs

1. Draw a pictograph on chart paper. Title the graph *Tickets Won*, and draw a key indicating each counter means 1 ticket. Label the rows *Corinna, Grace, Owen*, and *Travis*.
2. Have students place 5 counters on the row for Corinna, 3 for Grace, 6 for Owen, and 4 for Travis. Point out the key. Reinforce that each counter means 1 ticket. Counters do not touch one another so that they are recognized as 1 unit each. They should also be aligned in columns as well as rows.
3. Ask, "How many tickets does Grace have? What did you do to find your answer? Does any other student have 3 tickets? Which student has 4 tickets? How many students have more than 4 tickets? Who has the most tickets? How do you know without counting?"
4. Have students copy the pictograph in their math journals. Model how to write a summary sentence about the pictograph.

Group 2 ☐

Analyze Pictographs

1. Draw a table on chart paper titled *Home Runs Scored*. Include rows labeled for the following players and the number of home runs earned: Chloe (5), Hannah (4), Miguel (5), and Wyatt (6).
2. Draw a pictograph and include a key that shows 1 baseball equals 1 home run scored. Have volunteers use the information in the table to draw the correct number of baseballs next to each student.
3. Ask, "Which student earned the most home runs this season? How do you know? Who earned 4 home runs? How did you find your answer? Which two students earned 5 home runs? Who scored more home runs— Hannah or Wyatt? How many more? Why is the key important for the graph? How would the data change if each circle equaled 2 home runs scored?"
4. Have students copy the pictograph in their math journals and write three questions about the data.

Group 3 △

Interpret Pictographs

1. Draw a pictograph titled *Fall Birthdays* and include a key indicating each cake means 2 students. Label the rows *September, October, November,* and *December*.
2. Say, "Three students have a birthday in September. How can I show that on the pictograph?" Draw 1 cake and 1/2 of another. Explain that each cake means 2 students, so 1/2 of a cake means 1 student.
3. Say, "In October, there are 5 more birthdays than September. What do I do to find the total number of birthdays in October? How do I show that on the pictograph?" Have students draw the correct number of cakes on the pictograph.
4. Ask, "Why is the key important for the graph? How would the data change if each cake represented one birthday? How does increasing the number of students represented by each cake change the pictograph?"
5. Have students write in their math journals about how the key affects a pictograph display.

Name_____

Look at the graph. Answer the questions.

Free Throw Contest

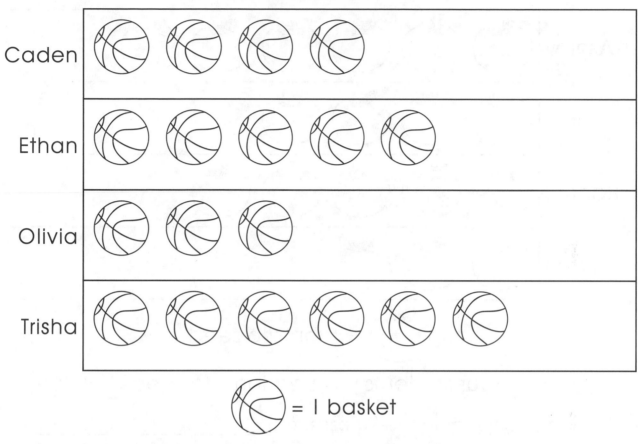

= 1 basket

Four students held a free throw contest.

1. What does each basketball in the graph mean? _____

2. Which student made the most baskets?_____

3. How many baskets did Ethan make? _____

4. Which student made 4 baskets? _____

5. How many baskets did Olivia and Caden make in all? _____

6. How many more baskets did Trisha make than Olivia? _____

Name_____

Look at the graph. Answer the questions.

Tomato Seeds Planted

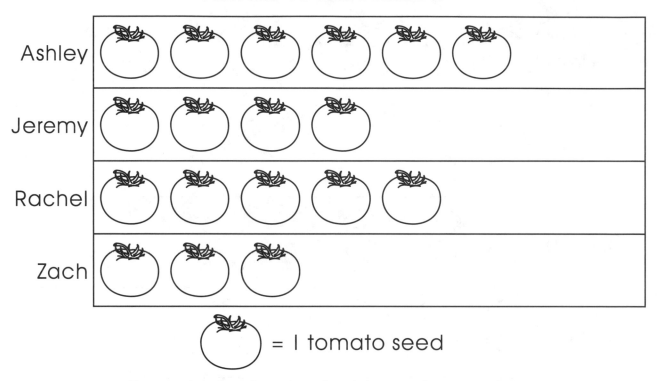

= 1 tomato seed

Four students planted tomato seeds.

1. Which student planted the most seeds?_____

2. How many seeds did Rachel plant? _____

3. Who planted more seeds—Jeremy or Zach? _____

4. Which student planted 3 tomato seeds? _____

5. How many more seeds did Ashley plant than Jeremy?_____

6. How many seeds did Jeremy and Rachel plant together?_____

7. How many more seeds did Ashley and Rachel plant than Jeremy and Zach? _____

8. What is the total number of seeds planted by this group of students?

_____

Name_____

Look at the graph. Answer the questions.

Books Read This Month

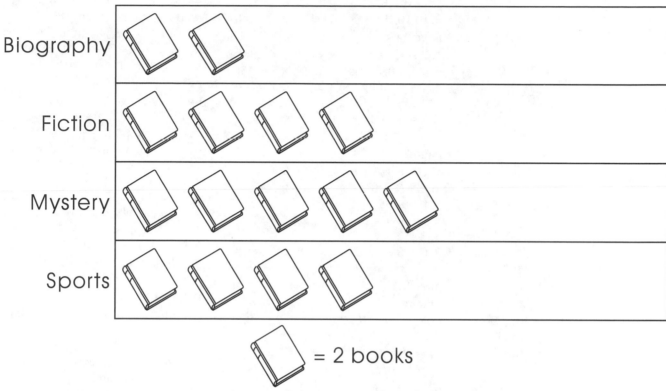

= 2 books

Henry kept track of the kinds of books he read this year.

1. Which kind of book did Henry read the most? _____

2. Which 2 kinds did he read the same number of? _____

3. How many biographies did Henry read? _____

4. How many more mystery books did he read than biographies?_____

5. Which kind of book did Henry read 7 of? _____

6. How many more fiction and sports books did he
   read than mysteries?_____

7. What is the total number of books Henry read this month? _____

8. How would the amounts change if each picture in the pictograph
   represented 1 book instead of 2 books read? _____

Answer Key

1. 7 tens + 3 ones; 2. 1 ten + 8 ones;
3. 2 hundreds + 4 tens + 9 ones;
4. 4 hundreds + 0 tens + 5 ones;
5. 3 hundreds + 1 ten + 7 ones;
6. 3 tens = 30; 7. 2 ones = 2;
8. 7 tens = 70; 9. 6 hundreds = 600;
10. 8 hundreds = 800

page 8
1. 30 + 7 = 37; 2. 40 + 2 = 42; 3. 100 + 50 + 4 = 154; 4. 200 + 10 + 8 = 218; 5. 500 + 3 = 503; 6. 300 + 70 = 370; 7. 400 + 10 + 9; 8. 200 + 80; 9. 700 + 30 + 5; 10. 600 + 7; 11. 935; 12. 408; 13. 312; 14. 860

page 9
1. 341 = 300 + 40 + 1; 2. 1,208 = 1,000 + 200 + 8; 3. 450 = 400 + 50; 4. 506 = 500 + 6; 5. 760; 6. 3,016; 7. 2,080; 8. 901; 9. 1,312

page 11
1. 29, 31; 31; 2. 54, 53; 54; 3. 60, 70; 70; 4. 30, 24; 30; 5. 115, 223; 223; 6. 68, 50; 7. 21, 27; 8. 34, 43

page 12
1. 64; 65; 2. 218; 223; 3. 430; 435; 4. >; 5. <; 6. >; 7. >; 8. <; 9. >; 10. 65, 561, 615; 11. 38, 308, 380; 12. 274, 427, 472

page 13
1. 58, 85, 95; 2. 25, 32, 53; 3. 147, 157, 174; 4. 304, 340, 430; 5. 509, 590, 591; 6. 76, 716, 761; 7. 49, 483, 487; 8. <; 9. >; 10. >; 11. <; 12. >, <; 13. <, <; 14. >, >

page 15
1. 79; 2. 88; 3. 55; 4. 52; 5. 95; 6. 90; 7. 58; 8. 83; 9. 121; 10. 165

page 16
1. $19 + 34 = $53; 2. $48 + 69 = $117; 3. $19 + 69 = $88; 4. $48 + 12 = $60; 5. $19 + 48 = $67; 6. $34 + 69 = $103; 7. $19 + 12 = $31; 8. $69 + 69 = $138

page 17
1. 178; 2. 134; 3. 100; 4. 868; 5. 398; 6. 352; 7. 1,108; 8. 2,127; 9. 3, 5; 10. 6, 7, 3; 11. 8, 4, 9; 12. 1, 9, 3

page 19
1. 34 − 16 = 18; 2. 61 − 29 = 32; 3. 28; 4. 14; 5. 27; 6. 39; 7. 23; 8. 16

page 20
1. 15; 2. 58; 3. 66; 4. 11; 5. 16; 6. 13; 7. 122; 8. 309; 9. 292; 10. 429; 11. 38; 12. 59

page 21
1. 81; 2. 52; 3. 179; 4. 64; 5. 448; 6. 73; 7. 90; 8. 85; 9. 287; 10. 976; 11. 300; 12. 141

page 23
1. H, 30; 2. E, 27; 3. A, 20; 4. D, 24; 5. G, 14; 6. C, 45; 7. J, 16; 8. L, 21; 9. B, 10; 10. F, 12; 11. I, 40; 12. K, 18

page 24
1. 2 sets of 3; 2 × 3 = 6; 2. 4 sets of 2; 4 × 2 = 8; 3. 3 sets of 5; 3 × 5 = 15; 4. 2 sets of 8; 2 × 8 = 16; 5. 4 sets of 3; 4 × 3 = 12; 6. 1 set of 7; 1 × 7 = 7; 7. 5 sets of 4; 5 × 4 = 20; 8. 5 sets of 2; 5 × 2 = 10

page 25
1. 6 + 6 + 6 + 6 = 24; 4 × 6 = 24; 2. 9 + 9 = 18; 2 × 9 = 18; 3. 5 + 5 + 5 = 15; 3 × 5 = 15; 4. 7 + 7 = 14; 2 × 7 = 14; 5. 9 + 9 + 9 = 27; 3 × 9 = 27; 6. 3 + 3 + 3 + 3 = 12; 4 × 3 = 12; 7. 6 + 6 = 12; 2 × 6 = 12; 8. 8 + 8 + 8 = 24; 3 × 8 = 24

page 27
The following numbers should be colored: 16, 18, 20, 22, 24, 26, 28, 30, 32, 34, 36, 38, 40, 42, 44

page 28
1. 50, 52, 54, 56; even; 2. 37, 39, 41, 43; odd; 3. 22, 24, 26, 28; even; 4. 75, 77, 79, 81; odd; 5. 66, 68, 70, 72; even; 6. 11, 13, 15, 17; odd; 7. 83, 85, 87, 89; odd; 8. 94, 96, 98, 100; even; 9. 19, 21, 23, 25, 27, 29; 10. 108, 106, 104, 102, 100, 98, 96; 11. 59, 57, 55, 53, 51; 12. 44, 46, 48, 50, 52, 54, 56

page 29
1. 85, 84, yes; 2. 28, 27, no; 3. 51, 50, yes; 4. 98, 99, no; 5. 63, 64, yes; 6. 915, 916, yes; 7. 14 headlights; 8. 24 socks; 9. 38 shoes

page 31
1. 15; 2. 40; 3. 35; 4. 35, 50; 5. 75, 85, 90, 100, 105; 6. 60, 65, 70, 80; 7. 135, 155, 160, 165; 8. 10, 15, 25, 30, 45, 50

page 32
1. 15; 2. 30; 3. 20; 4. 10; 5. 30, 35, 40, 45; 6. 85, 80, 75, 70; 7. 75, 80, 85, 90; 8. 35, 30, 25, 20

page 33
1. 2 × 5 = 10; 2. 3 × 5 = 15; 3. 6 × 5 = 30; 4. 5 × 5 = 25; 5. 30 seeds; 6. 25 slices of pizza

page 35
1. 4 groups of 3; 2. 3 groups of 3; 3. 5 groups of 2; 4. 2 groups of 6; 5. 3 groups of 4; 6. 4 groups of 4; 7. 6 groups of 4; 8. 5 groups of 4

page 36
1. 8 marbles in each plate, 24 − 3 − 3 − 3 − 3 − 3 − 3 − 3 − 3 = 0, 24 ÷ 3 = 8; 2. 5 marbles in each plate, 20 − 4 − 4 − 4 − 4 − 4 = 0, 20 ÷ 4 = 5; 3. 3 marbles in each plate, 18 − 6 − 6 − 6 = 0, 18 ÷ 6 = 3; 4. 3 marbles in each plate, 21 − 7 − 7 − 7 = 0, 21 ÷ 7 = 3; 5. 4 marbles in each plate, 32 − 8 − 8 − 8 − 8 = 0, 32 ÷ 8 = 4

page 37
1. 12 ÷ 6 = 2; 12 ÷ 2 = 6; 6 × 2 = 12; 2 × 6 = 12; 2. 20 ÷ 4 = 5; 20 ÷ 5 = 4; 4 × 5 = 20; 5 × 4 = 20; 3. 18 ÷ 3 = 6; 18 ÷ 6 = 3; 6 × 3 = 18; 3 × 6 = 18; 4. 24 ÷ 6 = 4; 24 ÷ 4 = 6; 6 × 4 = 24; 4 × 6 = 24; 5. 36 ÷ 9 = 4; 36 ÷ 4 = 9; 9 × 4 = 36; 4 × 9 = 36; 6. 14 ÷ 2 = 7; 14 ÷ 7 = 2; 2 × 7 = 14; 7 × 2 = 14; 7. 12 ÷ 3 = 4; 12 ÷ 4 = 3; 3 × 4 = 12; 4 × 3 = 12; 8. 28 ÷ 4 = 7; 28 ÷ 7 = 4; 4 × 7 = 28; 7 × 4 = 28

page 39
1. rectangle, octagon; 2. star, star, star, triangle; 3. square, diamond, arrow; 4. trapezoid, circle, circle, trapezoid; 5. octagon, triangle; 6. add star, square; 7. add circle, diamond, trapezoid; 8. add rectangle, triangle, rectangle

page 40
1. AB; 2. ABC; 3. ABCC; 4. AAB; 5. AABC; 6. AAAB; 7. ABBA; 8. ABBB; 9. ABCD; 10. ABAC

page 41
1. ☆ ; 2. ◯ ; 3. ▯ ; 4. ⬠ ; 5. ⬡ ; 6. ◇ ; 7. ◯ ; 8. △ ; 9. ⬠ ; 10. ☆

page 43
1. 18, 21, 24; 2. 21, 25, 29; 3. 7, 5, 3; 4. 20, 15, 10; 5. 18, 20, 22; 6. 32, 38, 44; 7. 13, 9, 5; 8. 31, 36, 41; 9. 13, 10, 7; 10. 15, 9, 3

page 44
1. 31, add 2; 2. 21, subtract 3; 3. 31, add 6; 4. 22, subtract 4; 5. 28, add 5; 6. 74, add 10; 7. 24, subtract 8; 8. 46, subtract 9; 9. 73, add 12; 10. 41, subtract 15; 11. 47, subtract 7; 12. 132, add 23

page 45
1. 41, 57, 61; 2. 26, 20, 12; 3. 47, 65, 74; 4. 46, 86, 96; 5. 88, 79, 76; 6. 50,

44, 38; 7. 23, 55, 63; 8. 32, 44, 58; 9. 27, 16, 3; 10. 125, 95, 60; 11. 64, 85, 109; 12. 38, 44, 51

page 47
1. add 1 balloon; 2. add 3 flowers; 3. subtract 2 triangles; 4. add 4 marbles; 5. subtract 1 heart; 6. subtract 3 stars

page 48
1. add 3; 2. subtract 4; 3. subtract 5; 4. add 2; 5. add 7; 6. subtract 6; 7. 3, 7, 11, 15, 19, 23; 8. 27, 24, 21, 18, 15, 12; 9. 71, 62, 53, 44, 35, 26; 10. 15, 21, 27, 33, 39, 45; 11. 19, 24, 29, 34, 39, 44; 12. 61, 54, 47, 40, 33, 26

page 49
1. – 4; 2. + 6; 3. – 5; 4. + 3; 5. + 10; 6–12. Answers will vary.

page 51
1. 10, e; 2. 11, c; 3. 5, f; 4. 8, a; 5. 16, d; 6. 16, b

page 52
1. 15 – 9 = 6; 2. 6 + 5 = 11; 3. 13 – 4 = 9; 4. 4 + 8 = 12; 5. 3 + 7 = 10; 6. 17 – 9 = 8 cards; 7. 15 + 12 = 27 salads; 8. 14 – 8 = 6 sunflowers

page 53
1. 12 ÷ 2 = 6, 2 × 6 = 12, 6 + 6 = 12; 2. 3 × 9 = 27, 27 ÷ 3 = 9, 9 + 18 = 27; 3. 15 ÷ 3 = 5, 5 × 3 = 15, 10 + 5 = 15, 15 – 5 = 10; 4. 3 × 6 = 18, 18 ÷ 3 = 6, 12 + 6 = 18, 18 – 12 = 6; 5. 28 ÷ 4 = 7 desks; 6. 8 × 10 = 80 pounds

page 55
1. 7; 2. 6; 3. 10; 4. 3; 5. 9; 6. 5; 7. 8; 8. 15; 9. 18; 10. 14

page 56
1. 8, 20 – 12 = 8; 2. 4, 27 – 23 = 4; 3. 5, 14 – 9 = 5; 4. 9, 41 – 32 = 9; 5. 6, 11 – 5 = 6; 6. 12, 25 – 13 = 12; 7. 7, 26 – 19 = 7; 8. 16, 8 + 8 = 16; 9. 22, 42 – 20 = 22; 10. 13, 30 – 17 = 13; 11. 34, 86 – 52 = 34; 12. 15, 24 – 9 = 15

page 57
1. box = 14; 2. triangle = 6; 3. circle = 5; 4. star = 9; 5. diamond = 12; 6. heart = 8; 7. hexagon = 7; 8. trapezoid = 4; 9. pentagon = 3; 10. oval = 6

page 59
1. 1 marble; 2. 4 marbles; 3. 5 marbles; 4. 1 marble; 5. 3 marbles; 6. 5 marbles; 7. 6 marbles; 8. 4 marbles

page 60
1. The roll of tape weighs more than the eraser.; 2. The watermelon slice weighs more than the cookie.; 3. The toy weighs less than the apple.; 4. You cannot accurately compare the weights of the key and button from the picture.; 5. The marker is heavier than the pencil.

page 61
1. marble; 2. paper clip; 3. milk gallon; 4. bean; 5. elephant; 6. unit cube (or paper clip); 7. book; 8. orange; 9. Answers will vary.

page 63
1. 3 in., 7 cm; 2. 1 in., 2 cm; 3. 5 in., 12 cm; 4. 4 in., 9 cm; 5. 2 in., 5 cm; 6. 3 in., 7 cm; 7. 5 in., 8 cm; 8. 4 in., 11 cm

page 64
1. 2 in.; 2. 4 cm; 3. 4 in.; 4. 3 in.; 5. 2 cm; 6. 3 cm

page 65
1–8. Check students' drawings.; 9. twice; 10. 0 times

page 67
1. A; 2. C; 3. E; 4. F; 5. D; 6. B

page 68
1. 5:30; 2. 7:15; 3. 3:45; 4. 9:00; 5. 11:45; 6. 4:15; 7. 2:45; 8. 6:00; 9. 8:30; 10. seven forty-five or quarter to eight; 11. ten thirty or half past ten; 12. twelve fifteen or quarter past twelve

page 69
1. 8:50; 10 × 5 = 50; 2. 1:40; 8 × 5 = 40; 3. 3:25; 5 × 5 = 25; 4. 15 minutes; 5. 45 minutes; 6. 30 minutes

page 71
1–6. The shapes should be colored correctly.

page 72
1. A, B, E, F, I; 2. D; 3. G; 4. D, H; 5. A, B, C, D, E, F, H, I; 6. H; 7. A, B, D, E, F, H, I; 8. A, I; 9. C, G; 10. A, B, C, D, E, F, G, H, I

page 73
1. , triangle, triangle;

2. square, rectangle (or triangle);

3. hexagon, trapezoid;

4. rhombus, triangle;

5. rectangle, rectangle;

6. square, triangle (or rectangle)

page 75
1. cylinder; 2. sphere; 3. rectangular prism; 4. triangular pyramid

page 76
1. cone; 2. cube, 6; 3. 6, 12; 4. triangular pyramid, 4, triangles, 6; 5. 2; 6. sphere, 0

page 77
1. cube; 2. cone; 3. square pyramid; 4. sphere; 5. rectangular prism; 6. cylinder

page 79
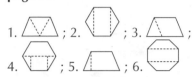

page 80
Check students' drawings.

page 81

1. ; 2. ; 3. ; 4. ; 5. ; 6.

page 83

Fruit	Tally Marks	Total Number
apple	卌 II	7
banana	卌 I	6
pear	IIII	4
pineapple	III	3

Sport	Tally Marks	Total Number
basketball	II	2
baseball	IIII	4
football	卌 I	6
soccer	卌 III	8

page 84

T-shirt Size	Tally Marks	Total Number
Small	卌 III	8
Medium	卌	5
Large	卌 卌 I	11

Game Outcome	Tally Marks	Total Number
Won	卌 卌 卌 III	18
Lost	卌 III	8
Tied	II	2

Travel Method	Tally Marks	Total Number
Bus	卌 卌 卌 卌 IIII	24
Car	卌 I	6
Walk	卌 I	6

page 85

Answers will vary.

page 87

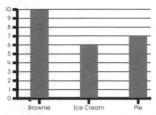

1. 7; 2. brownie; 3. ice cream; 4. 4;
5. 13; 6. 23

page 88

1. giraffe; 2. 7; 3. The number of
students is equal to the number in
between.; 4. The bar for the tiger is
taller than the bar for the panda, so
tiger was more popular.; 5. 4; 6. 13

page 89

1. vanilla; 2. 9; 3. 10; 4. 4; 5. 15;
6. The bars for butter pecan are the
shortest on both days, so it was the
least favorite.; 7. 21; 8. 5

page 91

1. one basket made; 2. Trisha; 3. 5;
4. Caden; 5. 7; 6. 3

page 92

1. Ashley; 2. 5; 3. Jeremy; 4. Zach;
5. 2; 6. 9; 7. 4; 8. 18

page 93

1. Mystery; 2. Fiction and Sports;
3. 4; 4. 6; 5. none; 6. 6; 7. 30; 8. Each
amount would be half of what it is.

CD-104562 © Carson-Dellosa